The Tivoli Murders

JOHN PILKINGTON

First published in 2021 by Sharpe Books.

CONTENTS

THE TIVOLI MURDERS

PROLOGUE

LONDON, 1891

They arrived late at night, having caught the last train up from Dover and, being unfamiliar with the city, wasted a lot of time finding a cabman to take them to Saffron Hill. Two men, bearded and dour-faced, in dark clothing that looked too heavy for an English autumn. After finding the address – a tumbledown terraced house, like all the others in this dimly-lit street - they knocked and, after some delay, the door was opened. As soon as they were inside the hallway, one closed the door while the other slammed the elderly householder against the wall and took him by the throat.

In no uncertain terms, he informed the frightened old man that he and his companion would be staying for an indefinite period, and would expect to be made comfortable and fed well. They would come and go as they pleased, and required complete discretion from their host. Failure in any of these areas would result in consequences he had best not imagine. Mention of their commander's name was enough to seal the arrangement; in fact, it caused the old man to sag at the knees, nodding vigorously.

'Be content, sirs - you can trust me!' He blurted, in his native language. 'I may be an exile but I'm loyal – always was and always will be! I would not fail to serve my true country…'

He broke off, his eyes flickering from one to the other, both men looking down at him with disdain. Finally they appeared satisfied, and between them hauled their wretched host to his feet. They were hungry and thirsty, they told him, and needed sustenance before retiring. And were there spirits in the house, worth drinking? Hastening to assure them that he had all they required, the other recovered himself and led them into a tiny kitchen that smelled of boiled fish, bidding them sit at his rickety table. Nothing was too much trouble, he said as he moved about, opening cupboards. Indeed, he was honoured to serve such men as they. They should let him know of any purchases he could make for them, in the morning when he went out to the market. Though he was a poor man, he added, with a quick glance round… likely they had been provided with funds?

He meant for their… he nearly said 'assignment', but changed it to 'their affairs' instead.

To that, the taller one – the leader, it appeared – replied that he would be well paid provided he did as they wished, which eased the atmosphere somewhat. The old man even managed a smile as he produced cups and a bottle. He knew better than to ask further questions; nor did he give any sign that he had noticed a slight bulge in the other one's overcoat, which suggested the presence of a revolver. It was not the first time he had been obliged to provide board and lodging for men like these – even if he was getting too old for such services, with the dangers they brought. Humming to himself, he found cheese and a loaf, and tried not to overhear the low conversation that passed between his guests.

None of the three had spoken English. The old man wondered briefly how these two would get by in the bustling city. Then, it was none of his business. And whatever theirs was, he prayed silently that it would be settled soon, and that they would then leave his house. Leave, or be killed in the attempted assassination - for their purpose could surely be nothing less.

As for their intended victim: that too, was none of his business.

ONE

It looked impossible – but then, that was how it was supposed to look.

Mind-reading: in their hearts, the watchers knew it was an illusion – what else was The Great Albertini famous for? One of the highest-paid magicians in London, rumour had it, if not in the entire country? And yet, illusion or not, no-one in the spellbound audience at the Daisy-Cup Music Hall could imagine how it was done.

Sam Vasey, watching from the wings, checked his watch: only ten minutes to go before they must hurry on to the next show. 'The Guvnor' was cutting it fine.

'Well now, this looks like a suitable specimen, sir. May I?'

The famous conjurer's voice boomed from the auditorium. Tall, suave and elegant as always in his white tie and tail coat, he leaned down to accept an object from a man in the front row. He had already scanned the crowd without their noticing, selecting suitable targets for his famous Psychometry trick. Some would have seen it before, of course, here or at one of the hundreds of other Music Halls around London. And yet, it never failed to amaze.

The object was a watch, which the man in the audience handed over eagerly, grinning at his companions. With a polite smile The Great Albertini held it aloft for all to see, scrutinised it closely, then turned towards the stage where his assistant, an attractive young woman known as Mirabel, sat on a chair blindfolded. Volunteers had already been invited to check the blindfold, and sworn that it was real.

'What am I holding, Mirabel?'

Gently the conjurer stroked the watch as it sat in the palm of his hand, closing his eyes in apparent concentration. Watched by the hushed audience, Mirabel tilted her head slightly but remained silent. Finally, as people began to grow restless, she spoke up clearly.

'It is a gentleman's fob-watch… a gold watch.'

There was a murmur from the crowd, and The Great Albertini smiled. 'Correct.' Swiftly he returned the watch to its admiring owner before taking a few steps along the row.

'Madam, may I trouble you?'

He had stopped before a woman in a large hat, who simpered at him. He indicated a brooch pinned to her dress, which she removed at once and handed over. Taking it in both hands, he again turned to the stage and asked Mirabel what it was he held. She paused for a moment, before nodding.

'I see an ornament… ceramic? No, a piece of jewellery… it's a brooch.'

Again the audience murmured in approval, but the magician wasn't done yet. Holding the brooch out to be inspected by those nearest, he kept his eyes on his assistant.

'And would you care to tell me its colour?'

Mirabel appeared to be concentrating hard. In the wings, Sam glanced at his watch again. There was the cabinet trick still to do… feeling a touch on his shoulder, he turned as Bradby Durrell came up.

'Ten minutes to go, by my reckoning,' he murmured.

'I know it - and so does he.' Sam threw a wry look at his driver, who was also props man and occasional on-stage assistant - even bodyguard, when the need arose.

'Keeping us on our toes, is he?' Bradby grunted. Both of them looked out at Mirabel, who now spoke up.

'It's blue,' she said loudly. 'A blue brooch… very fine, too.'

From the auditorium, the crowd let out a collective gasp before breaking into applause. Sam relaxed a little. He knew that the rest of the illusion would pass without a hitch, because it always did. The Great Albertini would take three further items from audience members – most likely a cigarette-case, a pocket-book, and a gold ring – which would duly be identified by Mirabel from the key words he used, which she had memorised. Then he would draw the trick to a halt and mount the stage again. He would remove the blindfold, allowing the 'mind-reader' to share in the applause while the orchestra struck up a flourish.

Meanwhile, a gaudily-decorated cabinet was being wheeled

into the wings by two stage hands. Sam nodded to them, then conferred with Bradby as to the arrangements. Their carriage was already standing by at the stage door, ready to hurry the company over the river to the Tivoli Palace of Varieties in the Strand. This small hall – the Daisy-Cup, in Southwark – was not one of Albertini's regular venues; there had been words between him and Sam, about the fee. Then, the great conjurer was rarely satisfied – in fact, there were times when he was downright impossible.

A lesser man than Sam Vasey might have left his service long ago, had The Great Albertini not been his father.

That was the best illusion of all, he sometimes thought: that the master magician, with his exotic airs, had been born plain Albert Vasey in the grimy suburb of Hoxton. At one time the notion would bring a smile to his features, at the way they had risen from obscurity to moments like this. But those days were gone; it was business now, pure and simple.

A sudden blare of music from the small orchestra, barely in tune, signalled the end of the mind-reading session. Soon the magician was back on the stage, savouring an enthusiastic burst of applause, cheers and whistles from the crowd. Striding over to Mirabel, he took her hand. His assistant stood up at once, allowed him to remove her blindfold and stepped forward to share the limelight.

'Ladies and Gentlemen!'

The voice of the Master of Ceremonies, his sweaty forehead shining through the clouds of tobacco smoke, broke the din. 'For your delight and delectation,' he cried, 'The Great Albertini will perform his final feat: The Enchanted Cabinet, from which anyone who goes inside will vanish! Your eyes – your very senses will be deceived! View, and be astonished!'

With a grand gesture, the MC threw his arm out towards the stage, where the chair had been whisked away to be replaced by the cabinet. It was the height of a wardrobe, on legs with iron castors. The Great Albertini stood beside it for a moment, before opening the door wide to show that the interior was empty. Mirabel, in her silver-spangled frock, stood at the other side. As the orchestra stopped playing, the conjurer raised his hands.

'Mirrors, I hear you say?' Surveying the crowd, who soon fell silent, he shook his head. 'No, my friends, I would not insult you with such tawdry tricks! Mirabel?' He turned to her. 'Will you oblige me by circling the cabinet, to furnish the proof?'

Mirabel did so at once, walking behind it so that all could see her legs, clad in black stockings, underneath its floor. Nor was there a trapdoor in the stage, as some might have suspected. As if anticipating the idea the conjurer bent down, thrust his arm underneath and thumped the boards. The Enchanted Cabinet was a box on legs, nothing more; and yet…

'My dear, if you will?'

As Mirabel came to his side Albertini straightened up and gestured, whereupon she lifted a dainty foot and stepped inside. As she turned to face the audience, the conjuror closed the door firmly. There were murmurs from the crowd, people craning forward in their seats to look. What few had expected, however, was the speed with which he opened the door again. It had been but a few seconds – and the effect was astounding: the cabinet was empty.

There were gasps, and voices rose, whereupon the conjurer called for silence. With a triumphant air, he walked briskly around the cabinet as Mirabel had done, allowing all to see his trouser legs and highly-polished shoes. Arriving at the front again, he seized it and swivelled it around on its castors, slapping the wooden sides. There could be no doubt: there was no hidden exit at the rear. The occupant of the Enchanted Cabinet had simply vanished.

'Are you mystified, my friends?' Albertini called out. 'Why, it's only magic! The magic of the ancients, taught to me by fakirs in Egypt. My assistant has but passed to another sphere, beyond your vision. But stay, for she will return at my command!'

He waited until the crowd quietened, before bowing his head; he appeared to be muttering an incantation of some kind. Then, with a grand flourish, he threw open the cabinet door once again – and there was Mirabel, filling the narrow space and smiling. As the crowd broke into applause, she stepped down onto the stage and spread her hands. The Great Albertini inclined his head, then turned to take his bow.

It was over; another Music Hall, another show… the orchestra burst into life, drowning the MC as he sang the praises of the master conjuror. Hand in hand, Albertini and Mirabel bowed again as stage hands hurried on to remove the Enchanted Cabinet. Then they were off, walking into the wings where Sam awaited them, nodding approval.

But all that his father said was: 'This place is a flea-pit. Let's get to the Tivoli – and fast.'

***

There were two cabinets. The one in which Mirabel had just vanished and reappeared would remain at the Daisy-Cup until Bradby collected it the next morning, along with various other properties, secured in locked cases. The other cabinet, of a similar design and construction, was already at the Tivoli, closely guarded by a stage hand tipped by Sam. It had to be this way whenever The Great Albertini did two shows in quick succession. As a rule, it took Bradby an hour to set everything up. During the hurried carriage-ride across Waterloo Bridge, in the chill air of the October night, the topic came up - as it was always going to do.

'I shan't go there again,' snapped Albert Vasey, who had shed his Great Albertini persona the moment they were in the carriage. 'The Tivoli crowd deserve my full attention… there was no need to book that dingy little hall beforehand. An audience of dimwits. Then, have we not trodden this ground before?' When his son, seated opposite him, made no reply, he persisted: 'Sam? For pity's sake, are you listening to me?'

'Of course, father,' Sam replied patiently. 'But let's postpone this discussion. You need to be fresh and alert for the Tivoli… the fee's handsome enough, isn't it?'

'I was not thinking of the fee,' Albert retorted. 'I'd expect nothing less, since the place re-opened. Downs is a man of taste, who recognises talent and rewards it accordingly.'

He named the Tivoli manager Edgar Downs, a long-time admirer of his. Sam gave a sigh, and kept his counsel. The carriage rattled along, cleared the north side of the bridge and was soon swerving into the Strand, Bradby handling the horses expertly in the evening traffic. Sitting beside Sam, the diminutive Mirabel had remained silent, muffled in her woollen coat. Now, putting on her sly look, she strove to lighten the atmosphere - as she often did.

'Keep your hair on, Alby,' she chirped. 'Or I might decide to stay disappeared next time I'm in the cabinet. That'd be a turn-up, eh? Make you fill your britches, that would.'

Sam hid a smile. No-one else could get away with talking to The Great Albertini as Mirabel did. Then, she was not Mirabel, any more than Albert Vasey was the celebrated Albertini, who claimed to have travelled the Mystic East learning age-old magic. She was Nancy Poole, a seaman's daughter from Limehouse, who had been a dancer before Sam spotted her at the Paragon Music Hall and suggested her as on-stage assistant. She would replace bad-tempered Maudie, who was due to be fired by Albert. Nancy had turned out to be a quick learner, with all the qualities the act needed.

'How dare you!' Albert replied indignantly, breaking Sam's train of thought. 'You're not so important as you think, you know. No-one's indis-'

'Indisputable?' Nancy finished, causing Sam to smile. 'Me, I'm indestructible. But not *indesirable*.' She grinned and fluttered her eyelashes.

There was a moment, before Albert gave in and merely threw his assistant a frosty look. He could rarely stay angry for long with Nancy. Thereafter the three of them – the great conjuror, his son and manager and their treasured assistant, sat in silence until with a clatter of hooves, the carriage lurched to a halt, the horses snorting in the shafts. They were outside the brightly-lit forefront of the Tivoli Palace of Varieties, across the Strand from the Adelphi. Cabs vied for space, drivers cursing and flailing their whips while crowds thronged the pavement, milling about the entrance. Sam and his father exchanged looks: it would be a good house.

Or so it should have been, had matters not turned out as they did.

***

Backstage at the Tivoli, all was bustle. The orchestra, much larger than the one at the Daisy-Cup, was in full flow, accompanying a popular singer whose shrill treble was clearly audible from the dim-lit passages. There were more than a dozen acts on the bill, among them singers, comics, a strongman and a juggler: an average night at this hall, which had been splendidly refurbished and re-opened to great excitement just three months previously. Making their way from the stage door to their dressing-room, weighed down with baggage, Sam and Nancy greeted those they knew: Benson the serio-comic, Florrie Bates the famous male impersonator, and the fine Swiss juggler Carl Brunner, who was practising in a corner. Then, to their delight, appeared the tiny figure of the American contortionist and human cannonball Mattie Burns, billed as 'The Triple-Jointed Terpsichorean Termagant'.

'Here we are again, my dears, ripe and rosy!' Mattie sang out, turning her wide smile from Nancy to Sam. A stranger might have taken meaning from it had Sam not known, as did most of the regular acts in the Halls, that Mattie flirted with everyone. 'Where's the Guvnor?'

'Talking to the manager,' Sam answered with a grin. 'Reminding him how important he is.'

'But so he is, Sammy,' Mattie replied, wagging a finger. 'You manage a race-horse, don't you know it? A thoroughbred – even if he is your pappy!'

Sam gave her a quick farewell and moved off towards the stairs. As he and Nancy were about to climb someone else came down in a hurry, almost colliding with them. Instead of excusing himself, the man scowled and waved them aside.

'Make way, Vasey. I'm on next, didn't you know?'

Sam frowned. Facing them was the comedian 'Cuddy' Carter: a hoot on the stage, but a notoriously sour fellow off it. Had those who laughed at his jokes ever met him personally, his star would have fallen long ago.

'How would we know it, Cuddy?' Nancy retorted, quick to react as always. 'You think we've got time to keep track? You're everywhere these days. You must need the money – lost on the horses again?'

'Watch your mouth, you little jilt,' Carter muttered. And he would have brushed past, had not Sam caught him by the sleeve of his garish checked jacket.

'No - you watch yours,' he said quietly. 'You're not speaking to her like that.'

'Oh - beg pardon, Sir Galahad,' the comic threw back. 'I was forgetting my manners. Then, I'm just a rough East End boy - not like you and your old man, eh?'

With a grin that was closer to a sneer, he jerked his arm free of Sam's grip and moved off. In the auditorium, the singer hit an ear-splitting high note to end her song, the orchestra came to a crescendo and a burst of applause followed. Nancy tapped Sam on the arm, signalling to him to leave the matter and take the stairs, when a familiar voice halted them both.

'What's this?' The Great Albertini called, coming up behind them, his coat over his arm and a cigarette dangling from his lips. 'Why aren't you in the dressing-room, getting ready? Must I see to everything myself?'

Without further word Sam and Nancy made their way upstairs, the Guvnor following. And soon, there was no time for squabbling. In the cluttered dressing-room costumes were donned and brushed down, props readied. The flowers – really dyed feathers, packed so tight that they barely filled the hidden pockets in Albert's coat – would be the first things to appear, seemingly from nowhere. The false vase was ready, a tiny rubber ball sealing the hole in its base, fixed to a thin strip of elastic which would draw a dozen silk streamers from his sleeve. There would be some further business with magic boxes, Albert improvising as he judged the crowd, before the Enchanted Cabinet appeared to crown the act. Bradby was down in the wings already, checking that all was in order.

Sam was about to remind Nancy about the tiny flaw in one of the hinged mirrors, which she must conceal with her arm before she pulled them tight, thus confining her in the secret, camouflaged triangle at the rear of the box. But as he opened his mouth, to everyone's consternation the door opened abruptly. No-one was supposed to disturb The Great Albertini before a show: it was common knowledge, strictly enforced by the management. Hence, with unease on the part of Nancy and outrage from the Guvnor, all three turned to see a well-dressed man with a clipped moustache enter, hat in hand.

'Mr Albertini, sir? I beg your pardon for the interruption, but I-'

'Good God, how dare you barge in here!' Albert's shout stopped the man in his tracks. 'Get out, before I have you thrown out! This room is private!'

'I know… my sincere apologies, but I would beg just a moment of your time,' the intruder replied, talking fast. 'I have a business proposition, which I feel sure-'

'Not now, sir.' Cutting the man short, Sam advanced towards him, hands forward. 'I don't know how you got in, but it won't do. If you have a genuine business offer, you should contact The Great Albertini by letter.'

'Of course - I would do so,' the man protested. 'But the matter is…'

Seeing that Sam was not someone to argue with, however, he faltered. Backing through the open doorway, he held up a hand. 'Please... it's a question of making me disappear, that's all – simple, for one of this man's skills. I'd pay handsomely… I'm not without funds, I swear-

But that was as far as he got before Sam steered him outside and closed the door. There was a bolt, which he had forgotten about. He drew it across quickly, preparing himself to receive a blast of reproach from The Great Albertini - whereupon Nancy disarmed them both by letting out a shout of laughter.

'Make me disappear?' she echoed. 'Well, that's a new one! Maybe you're wasting your time with me, Alby. You could start a new business, don't you see?' And as both men turned to her, she held up her hands as if displaying a street poster.

'On the run, are you?' she proclaimed, in a hawker's raucous voice. 'In debt, or are things going sour at home? Relax, we'll disappear you - for ever! Competitive prices – but no returns. Just step inside this cabinet, and-'

'That's enough! You add insult to injury!'

Albert silenced her, his cheeks reddening. But Sam felt laughter bubbling up, that would be hard to stifle. Of all things… drawing a deep breath, he looked away - whereupon there came a sudden knock on the door, loud and insistent. With a frown he turned round, while Nancy's grin faded. Albert, meanwhile, was about to roar his disapproval again – until a familiar voice from outside made all three of them start.

'Mr Vasey, will you admit me? John Chambers here… it's a matter of urgency. At once, if you please.'

Chambers was the Tivoli's stage manager, who knew better than anyone not to trouble The Great Albertini. It must indeed be urgent… with a glance at Albert, who gave a nod, Sam unbolted the door and threw it open. At once the man hurried in - and from his expression there could be no doubt that something was badly wrong.

'John, what on earth's the matter?' Albert demanded. 'Is there a fire?'

'No… no fire.' The man was somewhat out of breath from hurrying up the stairs. 'It's worse, in a way… but first, I have to tell you that the rest of the show is cancelled. The Tivoli must go dark for the rest of the evening-'

'What?' Albert broke in. 'You mean, we may not perform?'

'I'm afraid not. I can't stay now, for the crowd are restless… perhaps your man Durrell would lend us a hand, to restore order?' He glanced at Sam, who nodded at once.

'Of course - I'll come down too,' he answered. 'Has there been an accident, or…?

'Not exactly.' The stage manager lowered his gaze. 'Again, I'd say it's worse… excuse me, I must go.' And he would have hurried away, had Albert not stepped forward.

'One moment, please,' he said, his voice taut. 'Won't you at least give us a reason?'

There was a moment before the other raised his eyes, then shook his head helplessly.

'It's Brunner, the juggler… he's dead.'

The others reacted: Nancy put a hand to her mouth, while Albert blinked in amazement. Only Sam kept his composure.

'You said there was no accident?'

Again, Chambers shook his head. 'It's terrible. He's been killed – strangled, it appears.' And before the others could speak, he added: 'It's murder - right outside the Tivoli! Could you ever imagine such a thing?'

Then he was gone, leaving the door wide. In the distance, a commotion could now be heard.

It almost sounded like a riot.

TWO

Carl Brunner had been found lying in the alley at the rear of the Tivoli, where he had gone to smoke a cigar before he was due to perform. He had been discovered by a stagehand who had slipped out the back door to join him; smoking was not permitted backstage. The juggler's body, still clad in tights and spangled tunic, lay where it had fallen; no-one dared touch it. The police had been summoned, while the Tivoli staff were doing their best to clear the building and comfort the shocked performers, some of whom were in tears. Brunner had been a popular man: gentle by nature, with a modesty that belied his skills. Why, people said, it was unthinkable…

'By the look of him, I'd say his neck was broken by someone who knew their business.'

Bradby Durrell spoke calmly, standing with Sam, John Chambers and two stagehands. One of them, smoking nervously, was the young man who had stumbled upon the body.

'It's horrible,' he muttered. 'I saw him only minutes before he went out…' He broke off, putting the cigarette shakily to his lips.

'So did I, Billy,' Sam told him. 'It's a shock for us all - but worse for you, I'd say.'

'How do you know he was killed by someone… someone like that?' Chambers asked, looking hard at Bradby.

'Mr Durrell was a soldier,' Sam told him. 'He saw sights like this - and far worse, in the Sudan campaign. Though he doesn't talk about it as a rule.'

Bradby lowered his eyes, while Chambers sighed and looked away. From the Strand came the distant noise of traffic. The other stagehand, an older man, put a hand on Billy's shoulder.

'Shall I take the lad inside, sir?' He asked. 'Make him a mug of strong tea?'

'I suppose so,' the stage manager replied. 'I expect the police will want to speak to him…'

He broke off, and all of them turned at the sound of clattering hooves. A hansom cab was drawing up at the entrance to the alley, the door already swinging open. The person who stepped out, however, was no policeman. Having reached up to thrust a coin into the cabman's hand, he hurried towards the group, then stopped in his tracks.

'Paulo…?' Sam recognised Paulo Brunner, son of the deceased juggler. A handsome young man in bowler hat and well-cut suit, he threw Sam a fearful look.

'When did it happen?' He demanded. 'I've only now received the message…' Taking a step forward, he looked down as the others moved aside, peering at the body of his father. 'My God…' he swallowed. 'I didn't get the whole picture. Was it a fall, or…?'

'Mr Brunner.' John Chambers raised a hand. 'Will you come indoors, to the manager's office? We can talk there.'

Paulo met his eye, and gave a start. His gaze flew from Chambers to Sam, then to the shaky figure of Billy Bowes the stagehand, causing him to draw breath sharply.

'What is it?' He demanded, raising his voice. 'In God's name, what?'

'Let's go inside, Paulo,' Sam said, moving towards him. 'These men will watch over your father until the police arrive. There's nothing you can do here for the present.'

But the juggler's son ignored him. Looking aghast, he pushed past Sam and bent down on one knee beside the body. 'No, surely not…' his voice catching in his throat, he looked up. 'Tell me it isn't what I think…'

'Mr Brunner, please.'Chambers gestured towards the door. 'Will you come and take a glass of brandy-'

'Who found him?' Paulo broke in. 'Was it you?'

He was addressing Billy. 'It was, sir,' the boy answered. 'He was lying like that, when I came out. We were going to have a smoke, is all…' to the other men's embarrassment the boy appeared to be fighting back tears. 'I'll never forget it,' he added. 'Not so long as I live!'

'Get yourself inside, son,' Bradby said. 'I'll stay,' he added, turning to Sam.

His boss barely nodded; there seemed nothing more to say. And after a moment Paulo Brunner got to his feet, gazing down at the lifeless body.

Sam went to his side, and steered him to the door.

***

It was a subdued group who assembled soon after, in the well-furnished office of Edgar Downs, manager of the Tivoli. Downs was at his desk, while Paulo Brunner sat opposite him with head lowered, nursing a tumbler of brandy. Sam and John Chambers remained standing, with Billy Bowes seated nearby, still badly shaken. The Hall was quiet now, the audience gone. Little more had been said about the tragedy; it was inconceivable how the juggler came to lose his life in such a violent manner. No-one else was in the alley, Billy had said. An air of shock and disbelief filled the room, until an officer from the Metropolitan Police at last arrived, accompanied by a constable.

The officer, tall and heavily moustached, introduced himself as Inspector Henry Maskell. Having surveyed those present, he asked a few questions before fixing his gaze on Billy.

'So, you saw and heard nothing.No voices, no footsteps…?'

'No, sir,' Billy answered. 'I'd swear to it.'

'Did you examine the body?

'Well, no… first off, I just thought he'd fallen over. Though that was foolish, him being such a nimble fellow… or he was, I mean...'

'What then?' Maskell snapped. The other men stirred, but Billy seemed ready to talk.

'I spoke his name,' he said. 'When he didn't answer, I bent down… his eyes were open. I knew he was a goner… I've seen a dead man before, when my Pa went.'

The inspector grunted and glanced at his constable, who stood impassively by the door. Sam found himself forming a less than favourable opinion of Maskell. He glanced at Edgar Downs, who met his eye.

'I think my employee has told you all he can, inspector,' Downs said, in his gravelly voice. 'Might he be allowed to go?' Without waiting for an answer, he turned to Billy. 'Take tomorrow off, Bowes,' he said gruffly. 'Get some rest.'

'Well – I will allow it, but I may need to question him again,' Maskell said sharply. He signed to the constable to open the door. With a last look round, Billy got up quickly and left the room. No sooner was the door closed again, than the inspector bent his gaze upon Paulo.

'Can you think of any enemies the deceased may have had?' He asked abruptly.

A silence fell in which Sam, Chambers and Downs exchanged looks. But Paulo Brunner gave a start, his brow creasing into a frown.

'Not a blasted one!' He replied angrily. 'My father was a gentleman, admired and beloved wherever he went. Even after my mother died, he never complained – just worked harder than ever. He hadn't an enemy-'

'The matter is,' Maskell said, silencing him, 'whenever I hear someone say a victim hadn't an enemy in the world, I start to get suspicious. I never knew a man who hadn't enemies. Would you care to reflect further?'

'Inspector, this is intolerable.' Edgar Downs got to his feet, wearing a glare that would have silenced his entire staff in a moment. 'This young man has just lost his father, in the most dreadful circumstances…'

'I'm aware of that, sir,' Maskell said. 'But my task is to find the culprit, or culprits. No man gets strangled without a reason. Assuming it was strangulation…' His glance fell upon Sam. 'Haven't you and I met before?' He asked.

'I doubt it,' Sam said.

'I never forget faces,' the inspector persisted. 'Might I know your name?'

'It's Vasey. I manage The Great Albertini - the illusionist.'

'Do you, indeed?' The other raised his brows. 'Interesting. Did you know the deceased?'

'I did,' Sam replied. 'And as others have said, I thought him a good man-'

'Yes, yes,' Maskell broke in. 'Then, all you Music Hall types stick together, don't you?

'Inspector.' Briskly, Downs summoned the man's attention. 'Have you gathered enough information now? All of us have things to do…' Turning to Paulo, he said: 'The Tivoli will give you every assistance, Mr Brunner. Your father was a valued performer. We'll cover the funeral costs, and-'

'Well, so you should!'

The young man got to his feet, seemingly still smarting from Inspector Maskell's words. 'You ought to have had a doorman out the back, Downs,' he went on. 'Who knows what rogues and pickpockets might be about, in that alley? And as for enemies…' he faced Maskell. 'As it happens, one name does come to mind. He's a comic, always short of money. My father helped him out with a loan, a while back. When it wasn't repaid, he mentioned it – nothing more. But the fellow didn't like it. Swore at him… a nasty piece of work, that one.'

At once, all eyes were on Paulo. But even before the inspector demanded the name of this person, Sam knew it.

'He's Carter,' the young man replied. 'Known as Cuddy. The sort who'd sell his own grandmother – and laugh while he did it!'

***

It was past midnight before The Great Albertini and his company returned to the Vaseys' large house in Highgate, on the northern edge of suburban London. While Bradby attended to the horses, the others went inside. Despite the hour Alice, Albert's ageing housekeeper, was up and awaiting their return. Nancy went at once to the room that was kept for her whenever she needed to stay, saying she was very tired. Sam and his father, for their part, went to the parlour where Sam poured out two large glasses of whiskey. Alice had offered to make cocoa, but Albert declined and sent her to bed. Easing himself down into an armchair, he took the glass from Sam and let out a long breath.

'Well, we know one man who couldn't possibly have murdered Carl Brunner,' he said dryly. 'Cuddy Carter has the best excuse anyone could have: when it happened, he was on stage cracking his tired old jokes in front of a thousand people!'

Sitting down opposite him, Sam gave a nod. As he recalled the embarrassed look on Inspector Maskell's face, when John Chambers politely mentioned the fact of Carter's cast-iron alibi, he almost smiled. He took a drink, before his father spoke up again.

'I can imagine tomorrow's headlines, once the popular press gets hold of the story: *Famous juggler brutally slain, just before he goes on at the Tivoli. Is nothing sacred?*'

'Try and put it out of your mind now,' Sam told him. 'You need to sleep. We've a show tomorrow at the Star in Bermondsey, remember?'

'Ah… the Heavy-and-Light Chest.' Albert's brow creased. 'In the turmoil, I'd almost forgotten.'

'We could delay it if you like, save the try-out for next week…'

'Certainly not,' his father retorted. 'We've advertised a spectacular new trick, and the crowd will expect it. Once we know it's a winner, we take it up West - to the Alhambra, or the Tivoli.'

Sam didn't argue; both of them needed a good night's rest before facing the next day's work. The Heavy-and-Light Chest was a new illusion Albert he had been rehearsing, in the privacy of his outhouse where the props were stored. No-one outside the company had breathed a word about it, the world of stage magicians being one of ruthless competition, where some would not scruple to steal a trick and claim it as their own. If there was one thing The Great Albertini valued above all else, it was his hard-won reputation. And if there was one thing he feared, it was the threat of sabotage by rivals jealous of his success - of whom there were several.

'I'll go down to Bermondsey early,' Sam said. 'Make sure they've got the magnet installed. Bradby says everything should be ready.'

'It had better be,' Albert murmured, before taking another gulp of whiskey. 'There'll be spies among the crowd, you know – I'd bet my life on it.'

It was true enough. Sam recalled the time a new trick had been closely observed by a man in the wings, paid by another conjuror to find out how it was done. Before The Great Albertini could perform it at the famous Alhambra in Leicester Square, the same trick had appeared at another Hall two days later, ruining the spectacle. Though it could never be proven, the Vaseys knew perfectly well what had happened.

The conjuror's name was Lysander Hobbs.

'That scoundrel Hobbs, for one,' Albert said, as if he had read Sam's mind. 'He's back from America, you know… we'll have to be on our toes.'

'So I heard,' Sam said, suppressing a yawn. He had no wish to think about one of the most ruthless men in London's entertainment world.Hobbs, who had risen from humble beginnings like Albert, though in Manchester rather than London, had been his most annoying rival for years. 'But I also heard he's busy promoting other acts now… getting a little too old for the limelight, perhaps.'

'Not a bit of it,' Albert snorted. 'Too conceited… always was.'

They sat for a while, finishing their whiskeys. These moments of quiet relaxation after a performance had been part of their lives for more than a dozen years now, ever since the teenage Sam Vasey had begun assisting his father. The old days of poverty, of endless travelling, of playing in dingy provincial Halls, being booed and barracked by rowdy, drunken audiences… those were far behind them now. Even further back were the days when a young and hungry Albert Vasey, plucked from the crowd to assist in a trick, had talked his way into working for the French conjuror Baratin, who had treated him like a slave. Mention of those times was now banished from the fine house in Highgate, which Albert had purchased proudly with the proceeds of his first American tour. His only disappointment was that his wife, Sam's mother Ada, had not lived long enough to enjoy it.

'Damn it, there's another thing I'd forgotten,' Albert exclaimed, breaking Sam's reverie. 'There are only two dressing-rooms at The Star – men's and women's. Bradby will have to guard the props…' he frowned. 'We shouldn't be playing these downmarket halls, Sam.'

'It was your idea,' Sam reminded him. 'Try out the Heavy-and-Light trick well away from the West End, make sure there are no hitches. We've always done it.'

'Yes... well, maybe Lysander Hobbs isn't the only one getting a bit old for it all,' Albert said, with a sigh. It wasn't like him, Sam thought... had the tragic event at the Tivoli shaken him, more than he cared to admit?

'That's a load of old tosh, father,' he retorted. 'You're just tired. Get yourself to bed, and you'll be right as rain in the morning.'

'Well... perhaps.' Albert hauled himself to his feet. But as he turned to go out, an idea struck him.

'I'd bet twenty sovereigns that Carl Brunner had a past, you know,' he said. 'Private stuff... the sort you leave as far behind as you can.Who in our business doesn't? He always said he was from an acrobat family in Switzerland, but was it true? And why in God's name, would anyone want to murder him?'

Sam merely shook his head.

***

The next day, a Thursday, dawned cloudy and windy. The Great Albertini slept late as usual leaving Sam to look after business, like making calls on the new telephone they had installed in the small office off the hallway. Alice the housekeeper refused to go near the instrument, claiming it frightened her every time it rang. It had rung already, in fact, before the household were up, forcing her to answer it and tell the caller to try later.

'It's not a natural way to converse, Mister Sam,' she said, wearing her habitual, worried look. 'You can't hardly hear what anyone says down it, anyway. Sounds like they're in a bathtub.'

Seated at the breakfast table, Sam gave a shrug. 'It saves time and money, Alice. We're in the nineties now. Did you know they've opened up a telephone line across the English Channel? You can ring the operator and put a call in, all the way to Paris.'

'Lord above... that sounds like magic to me,' Alice said, lifting the teapot. 'Did your father have a hand in it? And do you want another cup?

Sam signalled no, picked up one of the newspapers that lay on the table and scanned the front page. There were the reports, as Albert had predicted. All of London, it seemed, was intrigued by the dreadful murder of Carl Brunner outside the Tivoli. But worse, was the readiness with which reporters drew comparisons with the terrible Whitechapel murders; then, it had been only three years back.

'I saw the headlines,' Alice said grimly. 'The Tivoli… that's where the Guvnor was playing, isn't it?'

'It is, but I'll ask you not to speak of it,' Sam answered. 'He's a bit shaken. We were among the last people to see the poor man before he died.'

'He was a foreigner, wasn't he?' Alice enquired, with a suspicious look.

Sam said nothing, but turned in his chair as footsteps sounded in the hall. Nancy came in, wrapped in her Chinese silk dressing-gown, looking as if she hadn't entirely woken up.

'Come and sit down, dear,' Alice said, looking her over. 'You've had a shock, haven't you? I'll pour you a cup.'

'I'll have coffee, Alice,' Nancy said. 'If there is any.'

'On the stove,' the housekeeper replied. 'Won't take a minute.' She bustled out, seemingly glad to leave the two of them alone.

'Are you well?' Sam asked, peering at her over the newspaper. 'Did you get some rest?'

'Some,' Nancy answered, sitting down beside him. 'Then, luckily for me, I never saw the body. What about you?'

'Enough,' Sam answered.

'That young man, Paulo – Carl Brunner's boy,' Nancy said, after a moment.

Sam lowered his newspaper. 'What about him?'

'He's not as sweet as he looks. Tried it on with me once, outside the Islington Empire. He wanted me to get into a cab with him… I gave him a slap, sent him off with a red face.'

'Why didn't you tell me?'

'Well, you had enough on your plate. We were running late, and the Guvnor was in a mood.' She shrugged. 'Goes with the job, sometimes.'

Sam let out a breath. 'Well, it shouldn't do. Promise you'll tell me if it happens again.' He paused. 'I don't know the man well, but I always thought he was a decent sort.'

'All twinkly eyes and cheeky grin,' Nancy said, before letting out a yawn. 'They're the ones you need to watch.'

She fell silent, gazing out of the window. In this highly respectable, tree-lined street of handsome villas, few residents knew that the famous conjuror The Great Albertini dwelt amongst them. And none at all knew where he came from – he, or any of his troupe. Nancy drew her gown about her, then looked up as Sam gave a start.

'Would you believe that?' He stared at the paper. 'The police have made an arrest, for the murder.'

'What, already? Who's been arrested?'

'It can't be… it's absurd.' He looked up. 'There's even a picture.'

He held out the newspaper. Nancy peered at it, then drew a breath. 'What – him? The man who wanted Alby to make him disappear? Well, strike me dead!'

The two of them gazed at the sketchy illustration of a man being manhandled by two police constables, a look of dismay on his face. There could be little doubt: he was the one who had blundered into The Great Albertini's dressing room the previous night, with his preposterous business offer.

Alice came in carrying the coffee pot, saw the looks on their faces and stopped. 'Now what's happened?' She demanded.

Neither of them bothered to answer.

THREE

That evening, at the Star Music Hall in Neckinger Street, Bermondsey, Albert Vasey flew into one of his famous tempers. It had come about because of the electro-magnet.

'I made it clear from the very start that it must be dead-centre, under the middle of the stage!' He ranted. 'Now you say it's half-way towards the wings – why's that?'

The three men stood backstage in a narrow passage lit by gas-jets. The stage manager, a scrawny little fellow named Coates, gulped and spread his hands. 'I gave instructions, sir… least, I thought I did. We're not used to specialities like yours, see-'

'No, you're still a spit-and-sawdust house, when all's said and done,' Albert threw back. 'A glorified tavern!'

Coates looked helplessly at Sam, who raised his hands in peace-making fashion; it was a familiar enough role for him. 'We've still got half an hour,' he said to his father. 'I'll go below with Bradby, find out what can be done. Are you coming too, Mr Coates?'

'Gladly,' the little man replied. 'Will you take a glass of something, sir?' He added, facing Albert. 'If you'd care to step next door, to the Star and Garter, I'll arrange-'

'I never drink before a performance,' Albert snapped. But he gave Sam a nod. 'See what you can do. I'll be in the men's changing room… I only hope there's room enough.'

With a disapproving look at Coates he turned on his heel, whereupon the stage manager hurried off in the other direction with Sam following. Soon they had descended into the stuffy space beneath the stage, where there was barely room to stand upright. Two men crouched in the dim light, inspecting a metal box attached to the boards overhead, the underside of the stage itself. One was Bradby, who looked round as Sam approached.

'We've unscrewed it, moved it a couple of feet and refixed it,' he said. 'It's not centre-stage, but it's close enough. The wire won't reach any further.' He gestured to the cable, which stretched from the electro-magnet to a bank of dry batteries by the wall. Unlike most of the great West End theatres, The Star had not installed electricity.

Sam peered at the device. 'It'll do. So long as the foot-switch is well hidden he can hit it.' He eyed Coates, who was looking relieved. 'One of your boys will stand by down here, won't he? Keep an eye on everything? We can't afford any hitch with the electrics.'

'You've got my word on it,' the stage manager replied. He glanced at the other man, a stagehand, who also appeared relieved. 'Should be a full house,' he added briskly. 'It seems a long time since we had The Great Albertini here.'

He grinned; the crisis seemed to be over, though Sam knew that, in truth, it had been no such thing. Somehow, between them he and Bradby always managed to solve any difficulties.

The fact was, the Heavy-and-Light trick was a simple enough illusion, to those in the know. Volunteers from the audience, two sturdy-looking men, would be invited on stage to examine the chest, which was about the size of a travelling-trunk, and to lift it. Being made of light wood, it was easy to move. When they lowered it and stood aside, The Great Albertini would then produce the 'magic' walnut, and place it inside the chest while addressing the crowd. The walnut came from a secret place in a far-off land, he would proclaim, and its power was vast: it now weighed more than the tree from which it was picked. To prove it, he would invite the men to try and lift the chest again. When they did so, of course, they were confounded: it was immoveable, no matter how hard they strained. The audience could see they weren't faking: under the lights, if all went well, sweat would appear on the brows of the volunteers, as they tried again to lift. What nobody knew was that the bottom of the chest was lined with a thin sheet of steel, painted to resemble wood. When the conjuror worked the concealed foot-switch, the steel was engaged by the electro-magnet underneath the stage, clamping it tight. After the magnet was switched off, thanks to some neat footwork by The Great Albertini, the chest could easily be lifted – finally by the conjuror himself, who would raise it above his head, ideally to gasps and applause from the crowd.

It had to work, Sam was thinking. Though eager to use any modern methods that became available, Albert was always wary, and never content until he had seen his audience spellbound.And he was determined to leave The Star's audience spellbound, before launching the trick in the West End. The posters were already being printed.

'Here, have a drink with me.' Sam took a florin from his pocket and gave it to the stagehand, who murmured his thanks. He and Bradby then left the cramped space and made their way back up the steps. The orchestra was playing, and backstage the next act was ready to go on. Sam greeted one or two people, then made his way to the dressing-rooms while Bradby went off to his other tasks.

He hadn't seen Nancy since the morning, but assumed she was getting changed. Outside the women's room, he was about to knock when there came a voice from the passage behind him - that of Mirabel herself.

'Sammy. I've been looking for you – where've you been?'

'I was under the stage,' Sam answered, turning in surprise: she was still wearing her outdoor clothes. 'Where've you been, more like?'

'I let Alby go on ahead… he was jumpy as a jelly all day. I wanted to clear my head, so I said I'd do some shopping and get a cab later.'

He eyed her: she seemed a little flustered, he thought. But summoning a grin, she added: 'And it's a good thing I did. There was a phone call after you went, from the police. Name of Maskell. Seems he rang up before, only Alice told him to call later, like he was some tradesman. He wasn't too pleased about it.'

'I can imagine,' Sam said. 'What did he want?'

'He wants you and Alby to go to Scotland Yard and *assist him with his investigation*,' Nancy replied, emphasising the phrase for effect. 'Stuffed shirt, if you ask me. I pretended to be your private secretary, said I'd pass the message on when it was convenient, but we were all very busy. He didn't like that much, either.'

'Nancy…' Sam raised his eyes. 'Maskell's an inspector – he's the one dealing with Carl Brunner's murder.'

'What? The one who came to the Tivoli?' Nancy blinked. 'Strike me! But then again, the line was so crackly, he could have been the Prime Minister for all I knew.'

'Well, it's done now.' Sam gave a sigh. 'If he was expecting us today, he's going to be disappointed. It'll have to be tomorrow – meanwhile, hadn't you better get ready?'

'Course… it won't take long.' The Great Albertini's treasured assistant reached up and pinched his cheek. 'Chin up, Sammy. Another show, another shilling, eh?'

Sam put on his wry look, and moved out of her way.

***

To the relief of the Albertini company, not to mention that of The Star Music Hall's management, the Heavy-and-Light illusion went off perfectly, and scored a roaring success.

In the end, it hadn't mattered a jot that the chest was somewhat to the side of the stage: it allowed The Great Albertini to stand dead-centre, his booming voice stilling the otherwise rowdy audience. Following singers, a red-faced comic and an impressionist who merely mimicked other comics, Albert went on to a hearty welcome. Ably assisted by Nancy, whose appearance drew lewd remarks from a few young men, he made even familiar tricks with feathers, streamers and magic boxes go down well. Finally, instead of the Enchanted Cabinet, he performed his climactic illusion featuring the walnut that weighed a ton, leaving the crowd agape. The volunteers – two muscular workmen from the nearby docks – had done sterling work without the least idea why, once the magic was done, the flimsy-looking chest was impossible to lift. The fact that they were local men, regular drinkers at the public house next door, made the business even more convincing.

Even Sam was impressed: there was no reason now why the trick shouldn't be a success anywhere. Standing in the night-time breeze at the rear of the Hall, he said so, and was relieved to see his father too in good spirits.

'Let's have supper - on me,' Albert said, turning to include Nancy who stood nearby. 'You've earned it, all of you… how about Barry's, in Charing Cross? I could eat a horse.'

'What about Bradby?' Sam said. 'If anyone's earned it, he has.'

'Yes, yes.' Albert looked round impatiently. 'Where's the carriage?'

'On its way,' Sam told him. 'By the by, there's been a message. I didn't want to bother you with it before. It seems we're needed at Scotland Yard.'

The great conjuror's face clouded. 'Are you serious?'

'It's to do with Carl Brunner's death… perhaps because we were among the last people to see him alive, or something.'

'Great God!' Albert exploded. 'We weren't witnesses to his murder, were we? What more can we tell them?'

'I think it best we show willing.'

'And the publicity can't hurt, can it?' Nancy put in, keeping a straight face.

'I don't need that sort of publicity,' Albert retorted.

'There's also been a development,' Sam said. 'I suppose you haven't looked at the papers?'

'You know I haven't - I've far too much to think about.' Albert eyed him suspiciously. 'What sort of development?'

'They've arrested a man for the murder, Alby,' Nancy told him. 'And I'll bet a month's wages you'll never guess who it is!'

***

The following morning at eleven o'clock The Great Albertini, together with his son and manager Mr Sam Vasey, were shown into a rather shabby little office in Scotland Yard, at the rear of the building overlooking the river. The sign on the door said *Inspector H. Maskell*, but it was another man, short and sturdy-looking, who got up from a cluttered desk and came forward to greet them. He introduced himself as Sergeant Drewe.

'Please sit down, gentlemen,' he invited. 'The inspector's been called upstairs… he'll be along soon.'

'I hope so,' Albert said frostily, remaining on his feet. 'I'm a busy man - and in any case, we told your inspector all we knew, back at the Tivoli.'

'So I understand, sir,' Drew replied calmly; he looked like the sort who rarely allowed himself to get flustered, which made a good first impression on Sam. 'The matter is-'

'There have been developments?' Albert finished, making no attempt to hide his impatience. 'Yes, I've seen the papers - you made an arrest.' He refrained from adding what he had since learned from Sam: that the man in custody was the one who had blundered into The Great Albertini's dressing-room, with the ludicrous request that he make him disappear.

'Well… the fact is, we made an arrest, and now we haven't,' the other replied, after a pause. He was looking somewhat embarrassed, Sam thought. Seating himself, he signalled to his father to do the same. A moment passed, before Drewe eyed them both and explained. It transpired that the arrested man, who went by the name of Harold Holcombe, had a solid alibi for the time of the murder. He had been loitering backstage at the Tivoli in full view of many people, from before Carl Brunner had gone outside for a smoke until after the body was found. In short, he couldn't possibly have committed the act.

Sam and his father took in the news in their own ways. Sam had mixed feelings, among them one of relief: somehow, he had found it difficult to see that nervous, dapper man as a murderer. Albert's mind, however, ran on different lines.

'Then why in heaven's name did you arrest the fellow in the first place?' He demanded, with a scornful look. 'And more, if this meeting is going to be a complete waste of my time, I'll have words for your Inspector Maskell-'

'Father, will you please calm down?'

Sam's tone was sharp: there were occasions when it had to be, and this was one of them. Catching his expression, Albert closed his mouth.

Facing Sergeant Drewe, Sam said: 'I don't believe you would have asked us to come down here for no reason,' he said. 'How can we be of help?'

Drewe gave a nod. 'I'll come to it, Mr Vasey. But first, I can tell you that the man was arrested because he's not unknown to the Metropolitan Police. Without going into too many details, he's one of those whose looks belie his true nature. He's been violent towards his wife, for one thing. Moreover, he bribed someone to let him in by the Tivoli's stage door, claiming acquaintance with one of the female performers, which turned out to be an exaggeration.' He paused, then: 'He also claimed he had important business with yourself, sir,' – this with a look at Albert. 'Was that also an exaggeration?'

'It's a complete fabrication,' Albert replied at once. 'The fellow must be mad.'

The sergeant barely shrugged. 'You meet all sorts in my job, sir,' he said, before turning to Sam. 'Nevertheless, we've had to let Holcombe go. But to answer your question, you had a conversation with him, I understand? Would you care to tell me of it?'

Sam nodded, and gave him a brief account of the man's arrival in the dressing-room two days ago, and what had followed. Then, when Drewe appeared satisfied, he voiced another thought. 'This female performer the man claimed to know - can you tell us who that is?'

'I don't see why not,' the sergeant replied. 'She's an American lady… a contortionist, I understand. Goes by the name of *The Terpsichorean* something-or-other-'

'What - Mattie Burns?' Albert broke in. 'Are you certain?'

Before the other could reply, however, the door opened. Both Vaseys turned to see Inspector Maskell enter, looking a little sheepish. At sight of them he stopped, forcing a polite nod.

'Mr Vasey… and the other Mr Vasey. I thank you for waiting...' He glanced at Drewe. 'I trust you've been acquainted with the position…'

'Your false arrest, inspector?' Albert broke in, with a sardonic look. 'Indeed we have. All a bit of a fiasco, isn't it?'

Maskell frowned, then quickly became officious. 'Our enquiries continue,' he said. 'Naturally, we need to gather all the relevant facts… anything new, sergeant?'

Drewe rose from his chair. 'These gentlemen have been quite helpful, sir,' he said stiffly. 'With your leave, I'll see them out.' He looked at Sam who stood up, followed by Albert. As they followed the sergeant to the door, The Great Albertini couldn't resist a parting shot.

'Why don't you come and see one of my performances, Maskell?' He asked, with a thin smile. 'Bring your wife, if you have one. I'd be willing to arrange free tickets.'

'Most kind of you, but I seldom visit the Music Halls myself,' Maskell replied, with a frown. 'Nor does my lady wife, though we're fond of the theatre. The proper theatre, that is… Mr Irving is a favourite.'

The great conjuror bristled, but allowed himself to be steered swiftly outside by Sam. They barely heard Maskell call after them, saying that he may need to talk further, before they were in the corridor following Sergeant Drewe's retreating back.

Once outside the front doors, however, instead of giving them goodbye, Drewe hesitated, regarding both men in turn. Albert was eager to be gone, but Sam caught his eye. Clearly, the sergeant had something on his mind.

'Let me be candid with you, sirs,' he said, after a moment. 'This case has got us all stumped – even the inspector, though he'd never admit it.'

'Is that so?' Albert raised an eyebrow. 'Well, I wish you luck.' And he would have turned away, had Sam not spoken up.

'It's certainly hit the headlines, hasn't it? Brunner was a popular man… I suppose your superiors are eager for an arrest?'

'What do you think?' Drewe replied. 'Given what happened three years ago, and no-one ever caught…' he looked away. 'The Tivoli may be a long way from Whitechapel, but people are easily frightened.'

Sam glanced at his father, who frowned slightly.

'And the Commissioner himself is taking an interest,' Drewe went on. 'Not to overstate it, but Sir Edward isn't a man you want to disappoint.' He named the head of the Metropolitan Police: Sir Edward Bradford, the fierce, one-armed ex-army officer.

'Well, I sympathise, sergeant,' Albert said. 'But I don't quite see why you want to share your difficulties with us.'

'It's just a notion of mine, sir,' Drewe replied. 'I'd value your co-operation, as a man so well-connected – I mean in the field of entertainment. In fact, I'd be grateful if you'd keep your eyes and ears open, let me know of any suspicions you may have. Do you follow?'

He looked pointedly at Sam, who showed his surprise. 'I

suppose so,' he answered. 'But are we to take it you suspect someone from our business – the Music Hall business - to be responsible for Carl Brunner's death? It's… well-'

'It's ridiculous,' his father finished, looking highly displeased. 'I can't think of anyone who would do such a wicked thing - even a rival juggler,' he added dryly. 'You're clutching at straws, Drewe.' He turned to face the street, stepped away and murmured something about finding a cab. The sergeant lowered his gaze, then looked up again at Sam.

'My father spoke truly, about being very busy,' Sam said mildly. 'He thinks of little else but his work… nevertheless, I'll do what I can. Though keeping my eyes and ears open, as you put it, is no more than I do anyway. It's part of my job.'

He held out his hand, which was shaken firmly by the other; his look of gratitude was enough. Whereupon they parted, Sam joining The Great Albertini by the roadside where a hansom was already drawing up.

***

That afternoon a visitor arrived at the Vasey house in Highgate, and proceeded to darken what had already been a somewhat trying day even further. To the surprise of all, the visitor was Paulo Brunner.

Sam was in the office, dealing with paperwork. The show that night was to be at the Canterbury in Lambeth, a familiar venue for the Vasey company. Albert was in the outhouse, running through a routine with Nancy. When the front doorbell rang Alice went to answer it, then came back down the hallway.

'Mr Sam?' She put her head round the door. 'There's a gentleman, says you know him. He didn't give his name. Shall I say you're busy?'

'No, I'll go.' With a sigh, Sam got up and went to the door, in waistcoat and shirt sleeves - and stopped at sight of the man he had last seen in Edgar Downs' office, in great distress.

'Paulo?'

'Your pardon, old fellow, but I'm…' The other hesitated, sweeping off his bowler hat. 'I was at a bit of a loose end. Had to get out of the house, with all that's going on. Can't sleep, you see… thought I'd, well…' he trailed off, looking ill-at-ease, which was unlike the man Sam knew – or thought he knew. In view of what Nancy had told him the evening before, he felt inclined to revise his opinion of Carl Brunner's handsome son.

'Well, come in,' he said, putting the thought aside. 'The housekeeper will be making tea soon… you look like you could do with a cup.' He stood back, whereupon relief showed on Paulo's features. Hat in hand, he came inside, stepping lightly.

'It's very good of you. No doubt you've a lot to do – a show tonight, perhaps?'

With a nod, Sam led him to the parlour and bade him sit down. 'I'll let my father know you're here,' he said. 'He'll take tea, I expect.'

Paulo sat down – somewhat nervously, Sam thought. Leaving him, he went to the kitchen and spoke to Alice, then left the house via the back door. The outhouse was not locked, so he went in and told Albert of the visitor.

'What on earth does he want?' The Great Albertini had been busy with a new vanishing trick, which involved a small cage and a stuffed cat. Nancy, sitting among a clutter of props and cases, made no remark.

'Company, perhaps,' Sam replied. 'It's time for tea, isn't it? Will you spare him half an hour?'

With a frown, Albert signalled assent and said they would take a break. Sam glanced at Nancy, half-expecting her to demur, but she stood up.

'I expect the poor bloke's at sixes and sevens just now,' she said. 'We'll cheer him up, eh?'

A short time later, however, when the true reason for Paulo Brunner's visit became clear, the great conjuror and his son were less than cheered.

The young man had looked embarrassed when Nancy appeared, but the two of them managed to make small talk for a while as they took tea. Albert said little, apart from expressing condolences for Paulo's tragic loss. The funeral, it transpired, was set for the following week – just close friends and acquaintances from the little Swiss community. The Tivoli management had been as good as their word, and were providing assistance. Though there was a great deal to be done…

After a while the visitor fell silent, staring down at the flowered carpet. When the silence grew awkward, Nancy rose and took her leave. As she left the room she glanced at Sam, conveying a notion he had formed already: Paulo wanted a private talk - men's talk. And no sooner had she gone than the truth duly emerged.

Paulo Brunner was penniless, he confessed: *stony broke*, in his words. His father, it appeared, had left serious debts - though at that, the Vaseys exchanged looks: there was little doubt in either of their minds who would have run up debts. And when both of them eyed the young man in silence, he drew a deep breath and made his request.

'You're the only person I could think of, Mr Vasey,' he blurted out. 'It's God's truth… otherwise I wouldn't dare come here, cap in hand like this. But I'm desperate – at my wits' end! I implore you, sir… my father knew you as a man of integrity - one of the best, he always said! So, what do you say? Will you help a man out, before he sinks into the depths?'

Whereupon he gulped, swallowed and made every effort to look as if he was on the verge of tears.

Except that his performance failed to fool either The Great Albertini or his son, for one moment.

FOUR

The Vaseys did not speak of Paulo again: there was a show to do, and as usual all else was set aside. It was Friday night and the Canterbury was crowded, the gallery spilling over with noisy Lambeth residents.

For this performance, Albert would finish with the Enchanted Cabinet: the Heavy-and-Light chest featuring the magic walnut would furnish a climactic finale to the act tomorrow – Saturday night – at the Tivoli. As expected, everything went without a hitch, Nancy disappearing and reappearing with her customary style and alacrity. Leaving The Great Albertini and his assistant in the dressing-room, Sam went backstage to help Bradby pack up the props. And there, they were interrupted by an unexpected arrival: none other than the man who had blundered into their company two nights before, been subsequently arrested on suspicion of murder and then released. At sight of him, Sam let out a groan.

'Mr Vasey, sir! Will you spare a moment? I promise not to waste your time…'

'Mr Holcombe – I hear that's your name?' Sam faced him squarely. 'I've nothing to say to you – and if you persist in troubling us, I'll be obliged to take steps to-'

'Please, I implore you!' Harold Holcombe, clutching his hat, looked most anxious. 'If you'll but hear my proposal, I guarantee you'll think differently-'

'You heard him, sir.' Bradby, who had been fastening one of the cases, cut the man short. Taking a step forward, which made the other flinch, he raised a hand. By now he had learned all he needed to about the intruder, and wasted no time in letting him see that he would have no difficulty in throwing him out. 'We're busy, and you're not wanted.'

A moment passed. From the auditorium the orchestra could be heard striking up some breezy linking music, as one act left the stage and another went on. Holcombe hesitated, glancing from Sam to Bradby and back, then:

'I'll pay you a hundred pounds to make me vanish,' he announced. 'In advance, of course. No-one will know how, and you'll never see me again.'

'That's a lot of money,' Sam said, after a moment. 'But I promise you The Great Albertini's answer will be the same – I'm telling you, as his manager.' He glanced at Bradby. 'In any case, surely you know that it's merely a trick?'

'Unless you're plain stupid,' Bradby put in.

'Of course I know it,' Holcombe said, ignoring the remark. 'But it fools the crowd every time, doesn't it? Besides, that's not your concern… all I ask is to be disappeared, then allowed to get off the stage without being seen. Surely your father could arrange that?' And when Sam frowned, he added: 'Yes, I know you're his son - I've made enquiries.'

'I think I've heard enough – *sir*,' Bradby muttered, stepping close to Holcombe. 'You're leaving – with my help or without, it's all the same to me.'

And he would have seized the man by the arm, had not Sam intervened.

'For pity's sake, Holcombe…' in spite of himself, he was curious. 'I never heard such a thing. Why in heaven's name are you so eager to disappear in this manner - I mean, in public? If you're on the run, why not just take a train for somewhere-'

'But it has to be public!' Speaking quickly, Holcombe eyed him. 'I want witnesses – plenty of them. I would be in the audience with my wife, and all your father has to do is ask for a volunteer, whereupon I'll be on my feet at once. Then I go up on the stage, enter the cabinet and he vanishes me - but I don't reappear. I can simply switch places with the young lady – Mirabel, isn't it? After that, all you need tell anyone is that you never saw me again. Of course, you'll need to instruct me on what to do, when I get inside the box…'

He stopped: Sam's expression, and Bradby's too, had changed entirely. They looked at each other, then at once broke into loud laughter. Crestfallen, Holcombe watched them.

'Your wife – so that's it!' Bradby spluttered. 'Well, why didn't you say? More to the point, if you're that desperate to leave her, why don't you just skedaddle?'

'And save yourself a hundred pounds,' Sam added, pulling out a handkerchief. 'Not that my father would do it in any case – it's quite absurd. I can't think what possessed you to make such an offer.' Controlling himself, he blew his nose loudly.

'Very well, laugh!' Suddenly Holcombe appeared to lose control, gripping the brim of his hat as if he would tear it in pieces. 'You don't know the half of it. When a man finds he's made a mistake in his marriage… when he finds himself in love with another, who promises happiness where there's been little but misery, what is he to do? What would you do?'

To that Sam and Bradby had no answer, but Holcombe wasn't finished.'Perhaps I was foolish,' he went on. 'Then, desire may drive a man to desperate measures…' he drew a breath. 'Have you never been in love, Mr Vasey?'

'If I have, I wouldn't discuss it with you,' Sam replied. As the thought struck him, he added: 'And from what I heard recently, I'd not be surprised to learn that your wife would be just as glad to be rid of you… maybe more so. Do you understand me?'

Holcombe's mouth tightened. Whereupon Bradby placed a hand on his arm, and this time Sam made no effort to stay him.

'I'll escort you out, sir,' he said. 'I don't expect we'll be seeing you again.'

***

The night, when the company returned to Highgate, there was a lively conversation in the Vasey parlour over glasses of whiskey for the men and port wine for Nancy. Bradby had been urged to come in and retell the tale of Harold Holcombe and his bizarre scheme to escape from his wife, for the benefit of the Guvnor and his assistant. But when he was done, however, the laughter was somewhat brief.

'The poor fellow,' Nancy said, which prompted quizzical looks from the others. 'I was talking to Mattie Burns a while back,' she added. 'We went shopping together yesterday – did I not tell you?'

'You did not,' Albert answered offhandedly. Recalling what Sergeant Drewe had told them that morning, neither he nor Sam were inclined to feel much sympathy for Holcombe.

'She beats him – Holcombe's wife, I mean,' Nancy said.

'She's built like a brick wall… no wonder he's so keen to get away.'

'Oh? From what we heard, it was the other way round,' Sam said. 'He's known to the police for violence towards her.'

'Maybe that's what she told them, and he was too ashamed to deny it,' Nancy countered.

'Well, knock me down with a feather - or even a magic walnut,' Bradby said, letting out a breath. 'I've heard of such men – and such women too, but I can't say I ever met one.'

'We're tougher than we look, Brad,' Nancy told him, raising her fist. 'Wait till we get the vote – then you'll see.'

'Good God, not that,' Albert exclaimed. 'Next thing, you'll want to be in parliament!'

'What a curious day it's been, though, has it not?' Sam put in. 'One man turns up begging for a loan, while another turns up later offering us a hefty fee. If Paulo Brunner was a conjuror with an Enchanted Cabinet, he and Holcombe could get together.'

But Albert looked away. Despite his disapproval, that afternoon Sam had made Paulo a small loan out of sympathy, at which the juggler's son had expressed effusive thanks.

'I heard something else lately,' Bradby said. 'Lysander Hobbs was badgering Carl Brunner, wanted him to join his agency, but he wouldn't. Seems Hobbs has already got Cuddy Carter on his books.'

Albert grimaced. 'They're welcome to each other. As for Hobbs, he's power-mad.'

'The police told us that Holcombe's acquainted with Mattie,' Sam said, turning to Nancy. 'Or so he claimed - is it true?'

'I don't know,' she replied. 'I think he's just a fan…stage-struck. A sad little man, really.'

The men took in her words without comment. And soon after, they began to speak of the morrow. It would be the most important show of the week, when the Heavy-and-Light illusion would launch at the Tivoli.

'There's a few old acquaintances on the bill,' Sam said. 'Florrie Bates - and Chen-Li. Haven't seen him for a while. But Downs likes to have a juggler in the show.'

'And they don't come much better than Chen-Li,' Bradby remarked. 'Even if he never gives anyone the time of day.'

Everyone knew the remarkable Chinese juggler, whose feats surpassed all others: even Carl Brunner, as skilled as he was, had readily admitted it. But the man was an enigma, never speaking a word on stage or even off it. Some thought him arrogant, others called him plain rude. Yet to see him perform was to forgive him, for his sheer talent. The man had no assistant, but travelled with his French wife who did the talking for both of them.

'I saw him balance a table on his chin, by one of its legs,' Bradby went on. 'There was a billiard cue on the opposite corner of the table, standing vertical, and a ball on the end of that. Even if it was flattened, or had a groove cut in it or whatever, it was still a dazzler. The crowd loved it - but applause doesn't seem to matter to him. He just bows and goes off.'

'He's an odd fellow, all right,' The Great Albertini allowed, somewhat drowsily, before sitting up abruptly. 'Here, surely you're not telling me he's top of the bill?'

The other three looked at each other, trying not to laugh. But the night was over, and soon they drained their glasses and rose to go to their beds. The prospect of a good show the next day had cheered them all, even after the recent tragedy of Brunner's death.

But none could have predicted what would follow, on that fateful Saturday at the Tivoli Palace of Varieties.

***

The house was packed, and not only with regular Tivoli-goers: some people had come out of mere curiosity, eager for news and gossip about the murder three days earlier. Newspaper vendors were on the pavement outside the Hall, along with chapmen selling hastily-printed pamphlets with lurid accounts of the demise of the juggler. There was a police presence in the Strand, and Edgar Downs had hired extra doormen, more to reassure the staff than for any other reason. Backstage there was a business-like air, acts greeting one another more warmly than usual out of an unspoken solidarity. No-one mentioned Carl

Brunner. Instead, there was a slight stir caused by the arrival of the taciturn Chen-Li, who as always went to his dressing-room without saying a word to anyone. Standing in the wings, while they watched the male impersonator Florence Bates, Bradby spoke of it to Sam.

'One thing's crossed my mind, about Mr Chen-Li,' he murmured. 'I'm not even sure he's Chinese. I know he looks the part, but has anyone ever seen him without his pigtail and make-up?'

'I wouldn't read anything into that,' Sam said. 'Some performers like to keep up their air of mystery.' He paused. 'Everyone's playing a part, aren't they? Even the Guvnor.'

Bradby said nothing; none of the Albertini troupe would ever have spoken publicly of Albert's humble beginnings: his hand-me-down days, as he called them. Moreover, all of them knew that one reason Sam's father and his arch-rival Lysander Hobbs detested one another was that they shared a similar background. Then, professional rivalry was a part of the world in which performers moved - be they conjurors or jugglers.

There was a sudden blare of brassy music, as Florence Bates came to the end of her act. While she took her bow to warm applause, the next turn was stepping into the wings. Sam glanced round, and his face fell: it was Cuddy Carter.

'You again, Vasey? Seems you turn up like a bad penny,' the comic snapped, adjusting his gaudy coat. 'And here's my old mate Captain Durrell,' he added, leering at Bradby. 'Or, now I think on it, I meant Private Durrell. How's tricks, soldier-boy?'

'I'm not your old mate – *mate*,' Bradby retorted. 'And I didn't see your name on the bill – down in the small print, was it?'

'That's a good one,' Carter said. 'I'll write it down... then again, maybe I won't.'

He turned away as Florence Bates left the stage and strode manfully into the wings in her top hat and tail coat. Once out of sight of the crowd, she eyed the three men and sighed.

'I'm plain worn out, gents,' she said. 'Anyone got a cigarette?'

Without a glance, Cuddy Carter swept roughly past her into the lights, to applause and cheers. Miss Bates looked round at him, then eyed the others. 'Manners don't cost anything, do they?' She enquired, with a wry look. 'Even for a tight-fisted sort like him.'

'Right enough, Miss Florrie,' Bradby said; he had always liked for the woman. 'I'd offer you a fag with pleasure, if it were allowed.'

'I'll have to pop out the back,' Florrie said – then her face fell. 'Oh, no I won't. What was I thinking of?'

The men lowered their eyes; after Brunner's murder, it seemed no-one wanted to step out into the alley again. It had become a place to avoid. On the stage, Cuddy Carter's ribald jokes were flying in rapid succession, bringing shouts of laughter.

'Well, I'd best go and unlace myself,' Florrie murmured, referring to the bindings that flattened her shape into male form. 'A pleasure to see you again, gents.'

Raising her top hat, she threw Sam and Bradby a grin before moving off. Stagehands were entering the wings carrying stands and hoops for the next act: Professor Pocket's Performing Dogs. Sam looked, and saw that one was Billy Bowes, who had stumbled upon Carl Brunner's body.

'Billy…' he gave the youth a nod. For his part, Bowles barely acknowledged him in return, but made a show of busying himself with the props. With a glance at each other, The Great Albertini's men moved aside. It was less than half an hour before the Guvnor took the stage, and everything had to be checked. Whereupon:

'Gentlemen.' John Chambers, the stage manager, appeared from backstage. 'Are you well? And what of The Great Albertini?'

'We're all well, John,' Sam told him. 'Ready to go. Bradby will take a quick look at the electro-magnet first.'

'Of course,' Chambers nodded briskly. 'I put my best electrician on the job – it should go like clockwork.' Moving closer, he lowered his tone. 'I hope you've been able to put the… the events of Wednesday night behind you. The fact is, everyone's a bit on edge.'

'But that's why we're here, sir,' Bradby said, to lift his spirits.

'Mr Albert will give the crowd a thrilling show, make them forget. Escape – that's what it's for, eh?'

'Yes… true enough,' Chambers replied, though he failed to hide the strain he was under. Here at the Tivoli, the tragedy was still raw. He turned away to the stagehands, chivvying them to make haste. Sam and Bradby left him, Bradby to descend to the under-stage while Sam went to The Great Albertini's dressing-room. He was striding along the passage when a door opened, and a woman clad in black silk stepped out abruptly.

'Oh… Monsieur Vasey, is it not?' She exclaimed. 'How do you do, sir?'

Sam halted, recognition dawning. 'I'm very well, madam - are you?'

Facing him was Louise Chen, the French wife of the famous juggler. A good-looking woman in her thirties, in the world of the Music Halls she was respected well enough, being entirely devoted to her husband and his career. Moreover, she was his voice: no-one ever got to speak to Chen-Li, or to interview him. Madame Chen, with her coal-black hair and charming Parisian accent, was manager, spokeswoman and guardian rolled into one.

'We are well… both of us.' She summoned a smile. 'I see The Great Albertini is a big attraction tonight, once again? I would like to stay and watch, but we must be away. A busy life is a good life - would you not agree?'

'I suppose so,' Sam said. For a moment he was almost tempted to make mention of Carl Brunner, but quickly decided against it. The two jugglers had been rivals, though without any real rancour between them. He confined himself to asking politely after Chen-Li.

'He prepares himself, monsieur. He likes time alone, to make concentration…' she hesitated, then to Sam's surprise added: 'It has taxed him, this week… I speak of the death. A loss that is so horrible. I pray for Brunner, every night.'

Sam gave a nod, whereupon Madame Chen moved off, allowing him to be on his way. He was still mulling over her words when he entered the dressing-room, to find Nancy half-dressed and Albert nowhere in sight.

'He wanted a cigarette,' she explained, jerking a thumb towards the door. 'Said he would slip out the back… he acts like nothing happened there. Nerves of steel, eh?'

'Nerves, right enough,' Sam answered. 'But not of steel. He's put the business out of his head, is all.'

'He's no need to fret though, has he?' Nancy said airily. 'He's always got you to do the worrying for him. Now, will you tighten my corset?'

Sam sighed, and did as he was bidden.

And a half hour later, The Great Albertini and Mirabel walked out on to the Tivoli stage, to a warm welcome.

***

The show went splendidly – until it didn't.

Troubles during a performance were almost unknown to the great illusionist: meticulous planning, long rehearsals and endless practice saw to that, as they had lifted him from obscurity to the illustrious position he now occupied among stage magicians. And yet there was a breath-catching moment towards the end of the act, when the mind-reading session hit a bump in its otherwise smooth progress.

This time, Albert did not go down among the audience: it was simply not practical at the Tivoli, with its large and crowded auditorium. Instead he invited volunteers on to the stage, where they were visible under the lights. While Mirabel sat in her chair blind-folded, the three guests stood to one side, ready to offer their personal items. The first, once again, was a man's watch, which Mirabel duly identified on hearing the code words *Well now, this looks like a suitable specimen, sir. May I?*

Following appreciative murmurs from the crowd, Albert moved to the second volunteer, a young woman, and invited her to lend him a handkerchief. The code this time was: *How nice - are these your initials*? After a dramatic pause, Mirabel informed the audience that she saw a piece of cloth… no, a lady's handkerchief, embroidered. Whereupon, after giving his assistant due praise, The Great Albertini stood before his last guest… and stiffened visibly.

Standing in the wings, Sam stiffened to. The volunteer – a bald, middle-aged man in a cheap suit - looked vaguely familiar, though he failed to place him. So had Albert, it seemed, when the man first came up on to the stage – but in any case, it was now too late.

'Here's my contribution, Mr Albertini sir,' the bald man said, loudly enough to be heard from the back of the auditorium. 'Let's see what Miss Mirabel makes of this!'

And to general astonishment, along with an intake of breath from everyone, he reached inside his coat and produced, of all things, a snake.

'Never fear, it's not real!' he added, turning to the crowd with a broad grin. 'Just a toy… belongs to my son. He loves it - I had to bribe him to get it off him!'

There was a moment then, which seemed to Sam to last a whole minute. But he was helpless, as was The Great Albertini. Drawing a breath, Albert eyed the man and shook his head. 'I'm sorry, sir,' he said, forcing a rueful smile, 'but I fear the… this object is quite unsuitable. Do you have something more, er-'

'More like what you usually pick?' The man finished, still speaking loudly. And now, Sam saw it: this was a performance, intended to spoil the illusion.

'No, sir!' Gathering his wits, Albert raised his voice to match the other's. 'I mean, something that you wear yourself - a personal item, as these other guests have already provided. You've said that this… the toy belongs to your son, and so it isn't yours. You follow me?' And with that he turned to the audience. 'You understand, my friends, do you not? Mirabel must feel the object's emanations, which come from its owner, in order to picture it in her mind. It's quite natural.'

But there was a stirring among the crowd. The notion arose that the great conjuror was refusing the toy snake because his assistant wouldn't be able to identify it, which aroused suspicion. A murmur grew – until to Sam's relief his father rose to the occasion. But then, he usually did.

'I must insist, sir!' He boomed, lifting a hand in dismissal. 'Something of your own, if you please – time presses, and we still have much to show, for your delight!'

'But I want you to use this,' the other insisted. His smile was forced, the teeth showing; even from a distance, Sam saw the hard look that lay beneath it.

'And I say I will not,' Albert replied firmly. 'Now, if you don't care to assist me further-'

'She can't do it, can she?' The belligerent fellow cried. 'What do you make of that, eh?' The last question was addressed to the audience, who were visibly restless now. Sam thought fast: if he could somehow get word to Nancy, they might yet manage the situation…

'That's enough!' On the stage, Albert strove to reaffirm his authority. 'I must ask you to leave, sir.' He turned to the other two volunteers, who were looking nervous. 'Thank you, my friends, if you'd kindly return to your seats…'

'Just a moment!'

To everyone's surprise, not least The Great Albertini's, his assistant Mirabel stood up quickly, raising her hands. Her voice, clear and strident as a man's, was so compelling that a hush followed. Whereupon she took a few steps towards the volunteers, then halted before the saboteur – for he was nothing less. The man showed unease, but stood his ground.

'The object is a toy… your son's, you say?' The still-blindfolded Nancy put her hands out, palms upward, and bowed her head as if concentrating hard. Finally, when the tension had risen alarmingly, she lifted her head.

'I see a snake,' she said. 'A vile thing… will you take it away, and yourself with it?'

There was a brief silence, which was followed by a roar from the crowd - of mingled laughter and plain admiration. Summoning his self-control, Albert pulled Nancy's blindfold away, as applause broke out. With equal presence of mind, the orchestra leader raised his baton and the band struck up a flourish.

It was over, and Nancy had saved the day.

The volunteers left the stage – including the bald-headed interloper, who seemed in a sudden hurry to make himself scarce. Hand in hand, Albert and Nancy took a bow, before the conjuror announced his final illusion, the much-anticipated Heavy-and-Light chest.

Mercifully, the trick went off as smoothly as clockwork, just as the stage manager had predicted, and was well received. After what had gone before, however, it was almost an anti-climax: Sam, standing taut in the wings, knew that tongues would be wagging, and the entertainment press would not fail to report the incident. When the conjuror's act finally came to its end, and the two performers left the stage, he could have embraced Albert from sheer relief. Instead he gave Nancy a hug, then drew back to face her.

'How on earth,' he began, 'did you know…?'

'Later,' Nancy said, somewhat sharply. 'Just now, I need a drink.'

'And you'll have one, my girl,' Albert broke in. He was breathing hard, but recovering. 'By God, that man's a swine – he's the snake, not his damned toy!' His anger was rising, which was a good sign. Sam put a hand on his shoulder, and steered him away as the orchestra played on.

But the three of them had taken only a few steps backstage, before a commotion arose.

First came a scream, followed by raised voices, then shouting. A stagehand appeared, running past them - and in seconds there was tumult. Somewhere a door banged, followed by more shouts. When another stagehand appeared, Sam grabbed his arm.

'What's happened?' he demanded.

The man swallowed, wet his lips… and the words came out in a burst.

'The Chinaman,' he breathed. 'Chen-Li - he's been shot dead!'

FIVE

It was terrible, it was shocking, and it was evil, the newspapers said. A killer was abroad – not in the dark and dirty streets of Whitechapel but in the well-lit thoroughfares of West London, close to the Strand. Here, a short distance from where he had given a thrilling performance at the Tivoli Palace of Varieties, the well-known juggler Chen-Li had been shot and killed while about to climb into a carriage. His wife was with him, but she was unhurt. Witnesses heard gunshots and reported a figure fleeing the scene on foot, but it seemed they were too frightened to give chase. Meanwhile, the manager of the Tivoli, Mr Edgar Downs, stated that the premises would go dark for two days out of respect for the deceased. His employees were greatly distressed, but ready to assist the police in their attempts to apprehend the fiend responsible…

'Fiend?' The Great Albertini, seated at his breakfast table, threw down the paper in disgust. 'I've other words for him.' He stared grimly at Sam, who had remained silent while his father read the report aloud.

'The widow… that poor woman,' Albert went on, with a shake of his head. 'Not only did she see it all – she could have been killed too. In God's name, why?'

'Why would anyone strangle Carl Brunner?' Sam said, meeting his eye. 'If I didn't know the truth of what's happened, I wouldn't believe it. Two such performers, murdered in the space of a week? Its-'

'Absurd?' Albert finished. 'Insane?' He let out a breath, picked up the cigarette which rested on an ashtray, and took a long puff. 'Or is there another Ripper at large, who hates foreigners?' He blew smoke out, then: 'Perhaps he simply hates jugglers.'

'Be facetious if you like, father,' Sam replied. 'I won't. I saw Madame Chen not long before he went on… I can hardly imagine what this will do to her.'

For a while, both of them brooded. Sam finished his coffee

while Albert smoked and scanned the papers. The previous night seemed like a blur now: a flurry of panic backstage while the audience, as yet unaware of the terrible event, left the Hall in high spirits. In fact, the gossip was mainly about the bald man with the snake, who had almost spoiled The Great Albertini's act. Today, when people picked up their newspapers, it would be a very different story.

Sam looked up as Alice came in, carrying a tray and looking even more worried than usual. She had heard the news, and was mortified. 'I shan't sleep properly, Mister Sam,' she said. 'Not until this murderer is caught. You don't think it could be… you know, what they're saying?'

'The same one who killed those women in Whitechapel?' Sam shook his head. 'No, I don't. Those victims were stabbed, while Brunner was strangled and Chen-Li was shot. It doesn't tally with what happened three years ago.'

'The only connection I can see, as I've said already, is that both Brunner and Chen-Li were foreigners as well as jugglers,' his father said. 'I don't envy the police their task.' He frowned. 'I wouldn't be surprised if that Maskell fellow comes sniffing around again. As if we had an inkling.'

Sam made no reply, but got up to go to the office. It was Sunday: a day off for the company. Nancy had gone home to the small flat she and her sister occupied in Islington, while Bradby was in the stable grooming Albert's carriage horses. It should have been a peaceful time, for rest and recuperation – but for Sam, it would be the start of a period of unusual activity.

A visitor arrived around mid-day, and brought news that, if not quite as devastating, was equally shocking. It now transpired that not only had Chen-Li lost his life, the previous night. Only a short distance away, another body was found: a well-dressed man, shot through the heart.

The victim was Harold Holcombe, who a few days before had begged The Great Albertini to make him disappear, in public.

***

Sergeant Drewe from the Metropolitan police was the unexpected visitor. He had taken it upon himself to come to the Vasey house without the orders – even, it appeared, without the knowledge – of his superior, Inspector Maskell.

'I beg pardon for the intrusion,' Drewe said. 'I'm out on a limb here, but…' he spread his hands. 'You'll understand that, in the circumstances, we must spare no pains to find answers.'

The three of them sat in the parlour, Sam and Albert in stunned silence. There was little doubt, Drewe informed them, that the person who shot Chen-Li was the same one who had shot Holcombe, barely a minute later. Why he would do so was not known, unless…

'He was a witness,' Sam said. His mind was working fast, and had been ever since the sergeant arrived with the grim news.

'My suspicion precisely,' Drewe said, with a nod. 'He was nearby, saw the incident and might have identified the gunman.' He paused, then: 'We're dealing with a ruthless killer. As cool-headed and as determined as any I've known.'

'But, sergeant…' Albert wore a pained look. 'This is a matter for your people. Naturally we would assist if we could, but none of our company saw anything untoward last night – nor did we on the night Brunner died, as we've already told. As for your suspicions that someone from the entertainment world could be involved, once again I assure you-'

'May I speak?' Sam said, cutting him short. Without waiting for answer, he faced Drewe. 'I share my father's opinion that nobody we know would do such a thing,' he said. 'But we've no performance booked until Tuesday evening, so I could spare you a few hours. I'll talk to people I know, see if I can learn anything. Will that help?'

'It would be a great help, Mr Vasey,' was the sergeant's reply.

'Sam…' Albert's pained look became a frown. 'Is that wise? You have much to do…'

'I'll work round it,' Sam told him. To the sergeant, he said: 'I knew Holcombe, if only slightly, though I barely knew Chen-Li. Then, few people did…' he eyed his father. 'Both men leave widows, don't they? The least we can do is offer what assistance we can.'

With a sigh, Albert lowered his gaze: he knew his son well enough not to argue further.

'Then I won't keep you any longer, gentlemen.' With a look

of approval at Sam, Drewe rose to take his leave. 'You know where to find me, sir,' he added. 'Send a message by telephone, or even a telegram if you like. In return, I'll keep you informed.' He paused. 'There will be inquests, of course, though there's little doubt about cause of death, in both cases. As for the unfortunate Mr Brunner…' he shook his head, and turned towards the door.

After he had left, Sam went to the stables to find Bradby. As his boss put his head round the door he looked up, caught his expression and put on an enquiring look.

'I'll be out and about, today and tomorrow,' Sam told him. 'Looks like I'm an honorary detective, for the present.'

'Part-time, I hope?' Bradby said. But Sam was already gone.

***

That evening, the popular male impersonator Miss Florence Bates was appearing at Gatti's Music Hall in Westminster Bridge Road, known to everyone as 'Gatti's under the Arches'. After the show, as she left the stage door accompanied by a boy weighed down with her voluminous baggage, she was surprised to find Mr Sam Vasey waiting, dressed in his brown ulster. There had been showers that afternoon, and the street was still wet.

'Well now, to what do I owe the pleasure?' She enquired, as Sam tipped his hat to her. In her fur coat and wide hat trimmed with lace, she was almost unrecognisable from her stage persona: just a well-dressed woman, heading homewards.

'Could we have a chat, Florrie?' Sam said. 'There are few people I know as well-connected as you - or as smart. The matter is, if you can believe it, I'm assisting the police.'

'Are you indeed?' The woman frowned. 'You mean, after all that's happened? Heavens above, why would you want to get mixed up in that?'

'Call it curiosity, with a touch of public-spiritedness thrown in,' Sam told her. 'But as it happens, I feel just a little bit ashamed.'

He was thinking of Harold Holcombe, and the look of anguish on his face when he had asked Sam if he'd ever been in love. Somehow, he was finding it hard to get the image out of his mind. 'Can I hail a cab for you?' He asked. 'We could talk in there.'

'I suppose we could,' Florrie agreed. 'But first, I'd better pay my pack-horse.'

She meant the boy, who was standing nearby, still weighted with cases. At a word from Miss Bates, however, his face lit up. Touching his cap, he set down his burden and received the proffered sixpence with thanks. As he trotted off, the lady smiled faintly.

'I once thought I'd like a son,' she said. 'Now I've left it too late. But then, half the country thinks I'm a man anyway.' She indicated the baggage. 'We'll let the cabman fetch those, shall we?'

A short time later the two of them were seated in the hansom, swaying slightly as the wet streets of South London swept by. It was a fairly short journey to Florrie's home in Lambeth, and Sam was keen to talk; she was a mine of information. But very soon, he found that she had no wish to dwell on the fearful events of the previous night.

'I won't speak of it,' she said. 'I try not to even think about it. It'd put me in a dark mood… the blue devils, that's what Mattie Burns calls it. You heard of that?'

'I promise not to go over that business,' Sam replied. 'I merely told the police I'd poke about a bit, see if anyone knows anything worth passing on.'

Florrie shook her head. 'I can't tell you anything. I know Louise, of course, Chen-Li's wife – I mean his widow.' She lowered her eyes. 'It's like a dream. Two men murdered, both of them jugglers… can you grasp it?'

'In fact, it was three men,' Sam said, after a moment. 'Did you not know?'

Florrie blinked. 'What do you mean?'

'You haven't heard, then? It was in the papers…'

'I haven't looked at them. Who's the other one?'

Sparing her the grisly details, which the papers had relished – the blood-soaked body of Harold Holcombe, sprawled across a pavement - Sam gave a short account of the man's death, and the likelihood that he had been a witness to the shooting of

Chen-Li. But before he could finish, Florrie stayed him.

'That stage-door fellow?' she exclaimed. 'Why, I've seen him often. He had a crush on Mattie Burns at one time… used to hang about wherever she was playing.'

'So I heard,' Sam said. 'It seems he shifted his affections elsewhere after that. Had plans to leave his wife, and run away with his lover.' He told her of Holcombe's hare-brained scheme to have The Great Albertini make him disappear, by means of the Enchanted Cabinet.

Florrie was half-flabbergasted, half-amused. 'I thought I'd heard everything,' she said. 'Now, I believe I'd swear to it.'

'He was a troubled fellow,' Sam murmured. 'Desperate, and clutching at straws.'

'He must have been.' She sighed. 'It takes all sorts, eh?'

'So, now that I've told you all, can you think of anything that might shed some light?' Sam asked. 'The fact is, the police think someone connected with the Halls might be involved – yes, I know.' At Florrie's expression, he nodded quickly. 'It's too dreadful to believe. But people are scared… there could even be panic. Do you see?'

'Well, I hadn't thought of it like that.' She frowned. 'Do you think they'll start shying away from the Halls – or at least, from the Tivoli?'

'I don't know,' Sam replied. 'And to be frank with you, I hadn't really thought of that either.'

***

The rest of the night, and the next day too, passed quickly. True to his word, Sam sought out friends and acquaintances from the Music Halls and asked them what they knew of the murdered men, as well as what they could remember from the nights when the killings had taken place. Yet, by the end of the Monday, he had to admit that he had learned very little. Shocked by the crimes, no-one he spoke to could think of a reason why anyone would shoot Chen-Li in cold blood, let alone strangle such a well-liked man as Carl Brunner. It was a mystery, some said, worthy of a penny-dreadful novel, or even a moralising tale: the sort of sermon given to young girls by stern fathers, about the dangers of going upon the stage.

At least, that was Cuddy Carter's opinion.

Sam's talk with him was short, as it was the one he had least relished. He caught up with the comic at the Royal Cambridge Music Hall in Shoreditch, his usual stamping ground. On the defensive from the start, Carter made it clear that he was in no mood to co-operate.

'In any case, Vasey, how is it your business?' He demanded with a scowl. 'Sticking your nose in… you know what I think? That since your old man became such a star, you've had ideas way above your station.'

'Can we set aside your opinion of me?' Sam said tersely. They were standing in the dressing-room Carter shared, though for the moment there were no others present. It had been a long day, and Sam's patience was running low. Then, this man would try anyone's temper. As briefly as he could, he spoke of agreeing to help the police with regard to the murders – but as soon as he mentioned Carl Brunner, Carter's back was up.

'You know that his son, that weaselly little bastard, had the nerve to accuse me?' He snapped, jabbing a finger at Sam. 'Just because I borrowed a few pounds off his pa. I had to account for myself to the flatfeet!' The comic puffed out his cheeks indignantly. 'Well, here's a snippet of information, now I think on it,' he added, with something close to a sneer. 'I'd hate to send you away disappointed. Did you know that Paulo hated his father like poison? I'll bet you didn't.'

Concealing his unease, Sam indicated that he did not know.

'Oh yes - it was their secret,' the comic went on. 'Devoted family, closer than ever since the wife died, butter wouldn't melt in their mouths and all the rest of it – well, I know better. The juggler was a decent sort, right enough, bailed me out when I was down on my luck, but…'

He hesitated - whereupon Sam spoke, more harshly than he intended. 'Soft touch, was he?'

'And what if he was?' Carter retorted. 'There's others he slipped a few pounds to, beside me. Fact is, he was too soft for his own good – certainly where that slimy son of his was concerned. Spent the money as fast as his old man could earn it. In the end, even he'd had enough. Things turned ugly… do you see now?'

Sam gazed at him. He saw clearly enough, and didn't like it. 'Surely you're not suggesting Paulo had anything to do with the-'

'Me? I'm not suggesting anything, Vasey,' the other threw back. 'You're the snooper, aren't you? I'm just helping you out. Now, are we done here?'

And that was the end of the comic's testimony.

The next morning, however, events took another turn, which would put the murders at the Tivoli into a somewhat different perspective.

***

Sam took the telephone call in the office, where he had been busy with Albert's performing schedule. That evening, the Tuesday, the show was to be at the Bedford Music Hall in Camden Town. So when the manager rang up, he assumed it was merely to confirm that all was arranged, particularly with regard to the electro-magnet under the stage.

But that was not the reason. Tonight's performance by The Great Albertini, the Bedford's manager informed, was cancelled. Most regretfully, he added, but as things were…

'What things would those be, sir?' Sam asked, keeping a level tone. He was dismayed: nobody had ever cancelled a performance before, apart from the time there had been a fire.

'It's nothing personal, Mr Vasey.' The manager's voice crackled down the phone. 'We merely feel… that is, the board of management feel, that an illusionist doesn't quite suit the bill at present. People need songs and laughter… jollity. These are trying times…'

'I beg pardon, but would this have anything to do with the unfortunate incident that occurred during The Great Albertini's act on Saturday night?' Sam broke in.

At once, the Bedford's manager strove to reassure him. 'Oh, no – nothing of the sort, sir, I promise you. I'm sure we'll engage The Great Albertini again, and soon. But I repeat, this is a rather trying time…'

'I thought we had a contract,' Sam said, still taking in the news. 'To cancel without good reason would be a grave breach…'

But he was cut short. 'I should have said,' the caller added, somewhat hastily, 'that we've had some difficulties with the magnet. Your man should have been here to help, but it's somewhat late now. I'm sure you understand, sir, but as I say…'

Upon which there seemed to be a lot of hissing on the line, and he was gone.

Sam went directly to the outhouse, where Albert and Nancy were still rehearsing the illusion involving the vanishing cat, and gave the news.

'Oh dear… still, nice to have a night off, eh?' Nancy said quickly, doubtless to forestall the expected outburst from the great conjuror. That, however, was a wasted effort.

'Good God - do you know, this has been at the back of my mind since Saturday…' Albert drew a breath, then exploded. 'I knew it was sabotage! We all did, didn't we? That snake-fellow was paid to ruin the mind-reading act! I'd like to get hold of him, the…' Fuming, he eyed each of the others in turn. 'And I just know I've seen him somewhere-'

'Yes, so you've said,' Nancy broke in dryly.

'And what if I have?' Albert demanded.

'She just wants you to forget about it,' Sam said. 'As do I - so will you try?' He gave a sigh. 'We'll have to put our heads together, think what to do until the business is forgotten. As it will be, and quickly,' he added. 'It's what happened afterwards that could bring the real danger.'

The other two looked puzzled, whereupon he laid out his fears, as Florrie Bates had done two days before: the threat of a possible panic.

'What?' Albert's anger was subsiding, but only a little. 'You mean, people would be afraid to go the Halls – afraid to go out? Ridiculous! Why, I wouldn't be surprised if some of them cash in on the murders! Especially in the East End – those lurid little playlets they put on…'

'Even so, we must face the facts,' Sam said. 'The Bedford manager was sorry, but evasive. He's not cancelling his entire show. I haven't heard of anyone doing that, apart from the Tivoli, the last two days. But he doesn't want us just now, and we must deal with it.'

'I suppose we could go East again,' Nancy put in. 'Mile End, Bermondsey… they're not so fussy.' She faced the Guvnor. 'You can still pull the crowds, Alby. Chin up, eh? It's only temporary.'

There was a moment while the Vaseys exchanged looks, but as so often, she had lifted Albert's spirits. He looked round, pulled up a chair and sat down. Sam threw Nancy a smile - then as the thought occurred, he spoke up.

'You never told us how you knew about the toy snake,' he said, glad to change the subject. 'With all that's happened since, I almost forgot. Did you move the blindfold, or…?'

But Nancy put on her knowing look. 'You'd have to ask Mirabel about that,' she replied. 'She's the mind-reader, not me.'

SIX

That same evening, rather against his better judgement, Sam took a cab down to The Strand and entered the Tivoli. Uncertain what to expect, he made his way backstage where he was relieved to find that the usual pre-performance bustle prevailed. Stagehands recognised him and nodded, though some hurried by without acknowledgement. By the time he ran into John Chambers, he was uneasy.

The stage manager, however, was more than uneasy: he was visibly tense.

'Mr Vasey… good to see you again, even if we're rather at sixes and sevens. We've been dark since Saturday, you know…'

'I know,' Sam said. 'And I'm – all of us, are sorry for your troubles. If there's any way in which we can help…?'

'Kind of you,' Chambers said briskly. 'Was there any special reason for your visit, or…?'

'Only to offer our support,' Sam said. 'And to say that my father's ready and eager to appear here again, just as soon as you like.'

'Of course…' the other looked away. 'I'm sure Mr Downs will get in touch.'

'It's just that…' Sam took a step forward. 'I've heard troubling rumours, John - about a possible panic. You'll know what I mean.'

The stage manager hesitated.: 'To be honest with you, we've heard them too,' he admitted. 'There have been letters - not all of them sympathetic.'

'People are easily alarmed,' Sam said, thinking of his conversation with Florrie Bates.

'It's worse than that,' Chambers had lowered his gaze, but now looked up: he knew Sam well enough. 'Some have gone so far as to say the Tivoli will be haunted by the spirits of those men, who had been on stage just before they were killed. We've even heard from someone offering to hold a séance.' He gave a sigh. 'Not that we see any fall in customer numbers – quite the reverse. But the situation's grave… Downs is troubled by it.'

Sam managed a nod. He had arrived with the intention of asking a few casual questions among the Tivoli staff – now, he realised, that was the last thing any of them would want. It was a rash idea; and soon after, he and the stage manager parted company with a handshake.

He returned home to find Albert sitting gloomily in the parlour, reading *The Strand* magazine and nursing a glass of his favourite malt. As Sam entered, he looked up.

'We should have been getting ready to go on at the Bedford, just now,' he murmured.

Sam poured himself a glass and joined him. 'It's not a disaster, father. Nobody else has cancelled, have they…' whereupon he caught the expression on Albert's face. 'Have they?'

'The Paragon,' Albert replied. 'They telephoned half an hour ago. That was to be tomorrow night's show – just twenty-four hours' notice, the swine! They claimed there was some re-scheduling difficulty… just a temporary matter. I didn't believe a word of it.'

Sam gave a sigh. 'I hope you didn't fly off the handle.'

'Of course I didn't. I was taken aback, is all.'

He looked at Sam, who frowned slightly. There was a look in his father's eye that he had rarely seen: one that was a little too close to fear. To Albert, the very idea that the act could be in jeopardy was too terrible to contemplate.

'I'll talk to the Paragon tomorrow, smooth things over,' Sam said. 'That business at the Tivoli was sabotage – I'm sure Downs understands. I saw Chambers this evening - he was edgy but he didn't mention cancellations. More important things on his mind, just now.'

They both fell silent. The deaths of Carl Brunner and Chen-Li, of course, overshadowed all else. Albert finished his drink, and said he would go to the outhouse to practise. Sam knew he would stay up late, working by gaslight until he was wearied and could sleep soundly.

To busy himself, he went to the office to answer

correspondence, telling Alice to have an early night. Poring over his paperwork, he barely noticed how the time had slipped by until he found himself yawning. He looked at his watch, saw that it was past eleven and rose from the desk, whereupon he was startled by the ringing of the doorbell.

In surprise at its lateness, and to forestall Alice having to rouse herself, he hurried out to the hallway and reached the front door just as the bell rang again – far too soon. Quickly, he unbolted it and opened it a short way, to find two people on the step, muffled in heavy coats. And yet, what startled him first was not the identity of the callers, whom he soon recognised, but the difference in their heights: one of them an elegant figure swathed from head to toe in black, who towered over the other person by almost a yard.

The former was Louise Chen, the widow of the recently murdered juggler, whom Sam had last seen at the Tivoli prior to the terrible event. The other was Mattie Burns.

'Sammy!' She breathed, somewhat excitedly. 'We sure hate to trouble you like this, but you're the one I thought of first - can we come in?'

Lost for words, Sam stood back and threw the door wide.

***

It was not, the household would learn, a courtesy call, or even a matter of business: it was a flight into sanctuary. That was how Sam would think of it later, long after Mattie and the other visitor had been brought into the Vasey's well-appointed lounge, where guests were normally received. Here the two women sat while Sam summoned Albert from the outhouse. When the great conjuror entered, without jacket or necktie, he was at first embarrassed, then somewhat nettled by the intrusion… until the reason for it began to emerge. Thereafter he and Sam waited, while Miss Burns accepted a glass of brandy.

Her companion Madame Chen, however, refused a drink with barely a movement of her head. She was veiled, and kept herself covered throughout the entire meeting. Nor did she utter a single word, from the moment of her arrival.

'You'll excuse Louise,' Mattie said, with a glance at her. 'You know what a shock she's had… but that's not why we've come.' She faced the two men, then: 'It gave me quite a turn when I saw her. I only went to offer prayers and sympathy…'

She broke off as the door opened. Alice appeared with a dressing-gown thrown over her night-dress, and stopped in her tracks. 'Will you be needing anything, Mr Albert?' She enquired, after moment. 'Tea? Or some cocoa?'

Albert looked from Mattie to Louise, who again made no reply. In fact, she seemed barely aware of her surroundings. Mattie, for her part, threw a smile at Alice and shook her head. 'We're fine, dear,' she said. 'Only… 'she turned to Albert. 'I haven't got to it yet, but do you have a spare room? Not for me, you understand…'

She jerked her head towards the juggler's widow, who merely stared at the floor. Albert was startled, whereupon Sam took charge.

'Of course,' he said. 'Alice, would you mind making up the top bedroom?'

Straight-faced, the housekeeper nodded and went out. As soon as the door was closed, Mattie breathed a sigh of relief. 'I knew this was the place to come,' she said. 'I thought of Florrie Bates, but she don't like visitors. I surely do thank you… we both do.'

'It no trouble,' Albert said, gathering his wits. 'Madame Chen is welcome to spend the night here… but won't you tell us more?'

Mattie took a moment before answering. 'If you don't mind, Mr Albertini, I'd rather wait a while,' she said quietly. 'Until… well, until I've got my breath back, you might say.'

Once again, she indicated the veiled figure of Louise. And thereafter, they waited in almost complete silence until Alice returned to say that the room was ready, and she would be pleased to show the lady upstairs.

***

'She said but one thing to me, before she clammed up.' Mattie said, when they were alone. '*They will come for me now - as they always do. I must flee, or I shall die here in London.*'

In surprise, the two men gazed at her.

'I thought she was in a shocked state, or something,' their diminutive guest went on. 'But she was scared out of her wits. Said something about leaving then and there – that nice house, with all her fancy things. I tried to talk to her, but she never spoke again.'

'Do you believe what she said?' Albert enquired, frowning. 'That she fears for her life?'

'Those words,' Sam said. '*They will come for me now*… I think I know what she meant, though I don't like the sound of it.' He eyed Mattie. 'Do you know?'

'I can't say I do,' Miss Burns answered.

'Well - she too was a witness.' Sam eyed Albert, who was looking uncomfortable. Seeing that Mattie did not understand, Sam told her of the death of Harold Holcombe, of which she had no knowledge. On hearing, she almost jumped in her chair.

'Oh, sweet Jesus!' she gasped. 'Poor Harold… that starstruck fellow… shot, you say?'

'Soon after Chen-Li was – because he saw who did it. That's what the police think.'

'Then… oh, my… the murderer might have shot Louise too, right then and there!' Mattie said, aghast.

'I suppose he was distracted… saw Holcombe, and wanted to silence him there and then.'

'But this is mere speculation – most sordid and gloomy, at that!'

Both Sam and Mattie turned sharply to Albert, who was agitated now. 'What's the use of going over that awful business?' He demanded, eyeing Sam. 'Whatever happened or didn't happen, Madame Chen is alive and safely under my roof – for the present, that is. Surely this is a matter for the police now? That is to say…' seeing the look on Sam's face he added quickly: 'The lady needs to be with people she knows, who can offer comfort - relatives, or close friends. We aren't…'

He stopped, for Mattie was shaking her head. 'She has no relatives here in England. In Paris maybe, but I don't think she's set to do any travelling just now. As for friends…' she shrugged. 'That would be me, I guess.'

'And us,' Sam said firmly. 'She can stay here as long as she needs to. Isn't that so, father?'

He was looking at Albert, who gave a sigh. 'Of course…' with an effort, he faced Mattie. 'You did the right thing, Miss Burns, in the circumstances. Though I must insist on informing the police. If our guest is in danger…' he trailed off, shaking his head.

Sam relaxed a little, then asked Mattie if she would like another drink. Now that her mission – for such it was – was completed, however, she appeared tired all of a sudden and said she preferred to go home. The offer of a bed for the night was declined. Whereupon Sam insisted on escorting her down to the main road and finding a cab.

With a grateful smile, the plucky woman agreed, and said her farewell to Albert. The Great Albertini saw them both to the door, then told Sam that he would retire.

A short time later, Sam helped Mattie into a hansom, promising to do what he could for Louise. Then, as he watched the vehicle pull away, he felt a weight on his shoulders: one that owed more to the arrival of their troubled guest than the cancellation of tomorrow's show at the Paragon Music Hall. The latter was something he could deal with; as for the former… he pulled his collar up against the night air, and turned briskly to walk home.

***

In the morning, Alice served breakfast more gloomily than usual. Sam and his father noticed, but refrained from commenting. Whereupon, after she had poured coffee, she waited until both of them looked up.

'Was there something you wished to say?' Albert enquired, wearing his bland look.

'It's the French lady,' Alice informed him. 'I knocked on her door, thinking I'd offer to take her some tea, but she didn't answer. So I put my head round to see if she was all right - and I got quite a shock, I can tell you. For one thing, the bed hadn't been slept in.'

'What – are you saying she's gone?' Sam asked sharply, but Alice shook her head.

'Not a bit of it, Mr Sam. If you can believe it, she was hiding in the wardrobe.'

'Good God,' Albert exclaimed. 'You mean, you heard noises, or…?'

'She was crying, sir,' Alice informed him. 'It was muffled – you wouldn't have heard it – but I knew where it came from. I opened the wardrobe door, and there she was – crouching like a child, wrapped in a blanket. Looked terrified, if you ask me. I asked if I could do anything for her, but she just pulled the door shut again.'

Sam and his father exchanged looks, whereupon Sam rose from his chair at once. 'I'll try and speak to her,' he said.

Alice went out, leaving them alone.

'Lord above, now what have we taken on?' Albert exclaimed, with a helpless look. 'The woman needs a doctor, I'd say. The shock has clearly been too much…'

'Perhaps,' Sam allowed. 'But let me try, will you? And before you remind me, I intend to telephone Sergeant Drewe and tell him what's happened… or most of it, that is.'

'Very well…' with a frown, Albert pushed the remains of his breakfast aside as if he had lost his appetite. 'Then will you speak to the Paragon? What a tiresome day it's turning into! And we still haven't perfected the disappearing cat…'

But since Sam was already through the door, he broke off.

After ascending the stairs, he arrived at the spare bedroom and knocked. When there was no reply, he opened the door slowly and took a step, then halted.

Louise Chen was sitting by the window, fully dressed and veiled. As he came in she turned sharply, but on recognising Sam looked away without breathing a word.

'Madam?' Sam took another step. 'Are you ill? Is there anything you require?'

There was no answer. He drew a breath, then without moving any further, raised his voice.

'You're safe here – I promise it. There's no need to come downstairs. I can have breakfast brought up here if you like, or some tea. Then when you feel ready, perhaps-'

'I want nothing.'

The words were spoken so softly, he could barely hear.

Feeling at a loss, he began to turn away, then paused. 'I understand, if you've no desire to talk,' he began. 'But please treat us as your friends. Will you do so?'

Yet the lady remained silent, whereupon Sam moved to the door. But before he had stepped out to the landing, there came a faint sound that checked him.

The lady was weeping quietly into her veil. Turning quickly, he saw her shoulders shaking, before she bowed her head. Already, it seemed, she had forgotten he was there.

***

By the afternoon, the atmosphere at the Highgate house had settled down a little, following the recent turn of events. Albert stayed in the outhouse rehearsing with Nancy, who had arrived in the mid-morning and been brought up to date with the news. Sam made his telephone calls: the first one to Scotland Yard, where he asked for Sergeant Drewe. The sergeant was away from his desk, he was told, but the message would be passed on. He then called the Paragon and spoke to the manager. It was an awkward conversation, but using his best diplomatic skills, he was able to secure a booking in a month's time, to make amends for the abrupt cancellation. He was willing to overlook the breach of contract, he said – which sealed the matter. Feeling relieved, he was about to go outside to inform Albert when Alice waylaid him in the hallway.

'Not to make a fuss, Mr Sam,' she said, stony-faced, 'but how long might the… your guest be staying? Only I'd like to know, for the groceries and such.'

'In fact, I can't say,' he replied. 'A few days, perhaps. You could order in for an extra person, and I'll inform you as soon as I can.'

'It's shocking, to see her like that, after what she's been through,' the housekeeper murmured. 'If you could get her to come down, perhaps…'

'I'll let you know,' Sam said patiently. He was about to move off, but Alice wasn't done.

'That tele-thing rang early, before you were up. I had to answer it, seeing there was no-one else. But when I picked it up, there was nobody there. Made me feel right uncomfortable.'

'It could have been a mistake by the operator. Or the caller gave a wrong number - you really shouldn't fret about every little thing.'

With barely a nod, Alice walked off to the kitchen while Sam went outside into a fine drizzle that was falling. When he entered the outhouse he was surprised to find Albert sitting alone, smoking a cigarette. At his enquiring look, the great conjuror waved a hand airily.

'She's gone for a walk. Said she needed some air.'

'In the rain?' Sam raised his eyebrows; Nancy was not known for taking walks.

'It's her choice,' his father said shortly.

'I came to say, the Paragon has rebooked for next month.'

'Well, I should think so,' Albert retorted. But he was relieved, and Sam saw it. Pulling up a chair, he began to speak of everyday matters. Since they had another night without a performance, Bradby had the evening off but would be back later to see to the horses. Meanwhile, they should think of using the Enchanted Cabinet the next night…

But quite soon, he fell silent: Albert was barely listening. Finally he turned, stubbed out his cigarette and faced his son.

'We should stay well out of all this, Sam,' he said. 'I mean the matter of Louise Chen's troubles. Helping a fellow artiste is one thing, but giving refuge to a woman who fears for her life is quite another. She should go to the police, or leave the country, perhaps. For all we know, whoever killed her husband might already be scouring London for her.' He shook his head. 'We could be putting ourselves in danger, don't you see?'

'Then what should we do?' Sam asked. 'Take her to a hotel somewhere, or…?'

'It isn't our affair!' Albert snapped. 'With these cancellations, we need to look to ourselves – sharpen up the Act, make people forget the business with that snake-wielding rogue.' He paused, then: 'Perhaps we should even think of finding an agent to make the bookings – yes, I know,' he added quickly, to forestall Sam's interruption. 'I've always refused to pay a commission to such men – and you do a fine job, no-one doubts that. But the strain is…' he hesitated. 'It weighs on all of us,' he added.

Sam, however, was not fooled by this argument for one moment.

'You've had a falling-out, haven't you,' he said wryly. 'You and Nancy – what was it about this time?' And when The Great Albertini looked away, he added: 'A serious one, then?'

'By God, but she's a headstrong woman,' was all his father said.

'She's also the best Mirabel you've ever had,' Sam replied. 'Remember muddle-headed Ellen – not to mention bad-tempered Maudie? Nancy saved the day the other night, though I still don't know how.' He drew a breath. 'We'd be much the poorer without her...'

'Yes, yes,' Albert broke in irritably. Then he sighed, and added: 'Of course you're right, as usual. And so was she, as usual. So the outcome is – the disappearing cat routine is out! Dead and gone, abandoned, thrown out with the cinders! You understand me?'

'So that's it,' Sam said, after a moment.

'Yes, that's it!' His father grunted. 'And if I ever suspected it wasn't going to work, I still assumed that trial and error – sheer toil and effort – would prevail in the end. But she wouldn't have it, and-'

'She told you so, and you had a row,' Sam finished. 'But think: which of the previous Mirabels would have dared stand up to you like that? It seems to me you ought to thank her.'

Albert made no reply, merely sat frowning in his chair. But he was calming – moreover, he knew that Sam was right. In relief, Sam was about to turn the conversation to business matters, when the door creaked open. Both of them looked round, hoping that Nancy had returned – but it was Alice, her head covered with a shawl against the rain.

'I've had to answer that tele-thing again,' she announced, slightly out of breath. 'Seeing I was on my own. You're wanted, Mr Sam - by the manager.'

'Which manager?' Sam asked at once, getting to his feet. 'Did you not ask?'

'I didn't have to,' Alice replied. 'He was a gabbler – from the Daisy-Cup Music Hall, he said - typical South London fly-type,

I'd say. He wants to talk about a show…'

But she trailed off, as Sam hurried out of the building. Turning to Albert, she was taken aback to see him lift his hands in apparent dismay.

'That damned flea-pit,' he said. 'Word has got round already, about the cancellations – they're just cashing in! D'you see?'

Alice nodded gravely, though she didn't see at all.

SEVEN

It was not ideal, but when all was said and done, it was a relief. The manager of the Daisy-Cup in Southwark, having heard about the Heavy-and-Light illusion that was such a success, was eager to book The Great Albertini – not at some time in the future, but that very night.

He apologised to Sam for the short notice; one act had pulled out through illness, he said, while another wasn't ready to top the bill, in his opinion - but The Great Albertini could. The Daisy-Cup crowd had yet to see the trick with the magic walnut, and they would love it. With Mr Vasey's approval, his people were pasting up new bills, even as they spoke…

It was fine, Sam told him, provided the fee was an improvement on last time. Though pleased, he had kept his presence of mind and talked business. As it happened, The Great Albertini was free, though it would be difficult to gather the company in such short order…

But agreement was soon reached. So the Albertini company were assembled at speed, once Nancy had returned from her walk which, it turned out, had merely involved drinking tea in a Highgate café. Bradby was despatched to Southwark with the props, especially the electro-magnet which would have to be installed in haste.

Albert, for his part, began fretting over details from the moment he, Sam and Nancy had taken a cab and were trotting down the Holloway Road in the drizzle. By the time they arrived at the Daisy-Cup, with the evening's show already in full swing, he was as taut as a walking-stick.

'I want you to remain on stage during the Heavy-and-Light business,' he told Nancy. 'You can hand me the walnut, take it out of one of the painted boxes very carefully. It'll add to the mystery. Apply due gravity, when you show it to the crowd.'

'Due gravity – what the blazes is that?' Nancy gave a snort; it appeared she had still not entirely forgiven her employer for the hard words that had passed between them. But when Albert opened his mouth to reply, she cut him short.

'I know… have I ever failed to put a face on? You'd best worry about your precious magnet.'

For some time after that nothing more was said. And a short while later, the two of them were installed in the same tiny, none-too-clean dressing-room they had occupied the last time, while Sam hurried down to the under-stage. To his satisfaction, Bradby had installed the magnet and connected the foot-switch, drilling a hole in the stage for the cable. Batteries had been found at short notice and all was ready, a stagehand standing by to keep watch. Soon afterwards, the two men stood near the wings while on stage an eager young comic fired jokes at the rowdy audience, with increasing desperation.

'Half of this lot are drunk,' Bradby remarked. 'The Guvnor needs to be careful when he asks for volunteers… maybe I should be one of them.'

'It's a good idea,' Sam said. 'Though as usual, I'll have to persuade him.'

'What's been going on, at Highgate?' The other asked, facing him squarely. 'Seems I only got half the story, before I left.'

Sam brought him up to date with the events, prompting a frown.

'That's a turn-up… what are you going to do with the woman?'

'I wish I knew,' Sam replied. A thought struck him: it was Wednesday - one week since Carl Brunner had been killed outside the Tivoli. Seven days that had badly shaken the company – indeed, with the subsequent death of Chen-Li, the entire Music Hall community. Mulling it over, he vaguely heard the small orchestra blaring out a link, until the young comic hurried by him, muttering something under his breath.

It sounded like: 'Sod the lot of 'em – I shan't come here again!'

Then Sam remembered: those were the words Albert had used following his last appearance here. Like most of the Guvnor's threats, it had proved to be somewhat empty.

***

On this mid-week night, when a full house was rare at the

Daisy-Cup, The Great Albertini would cause a minor storm: not because the Act was a great success – which it was, for the most part – but for what happened at its climax. Afterwards, the company would find itself in more trouble than even Albert at his most anxious could have imagined.

It began with the volunteers, who came up to lift the chest containing the magic walnut. One of them was Bradby: erring on the side of caution, Albert had agreed that he would be called up from the crowd, none of whom would know him. The other man, whoever he might be, was of less importance: drunk or sober, he would be unable to lift the chest once the magnet was engaged. With this added precaution, The Great Albertini had risen splendidly to the occasion, holding the crowd spellbound with his tricks: the vase and streamers, the flowers, the magic boxes, all wielded with his customary skill and flair. For good measure he had revived an old favourite: a flaming torch that appeared seemingly from nowhere, bringing a gasp from several hundred throats. Nobody saw the specially-made bulb that covered the pre-lit flame, before it was whisked into a hidden pocket in his coat. The crowd liked it, and despite their unruliness, were eager to see the much-trumpeted Heavy-and-Light trick. And quite soon, it was time.

When the chest appeared, carried by stage hands, there were murmurs of approval. After seeing it set down in the correct place, Albert allowed the master of ceremonies to announce the illusion with his usual energy. Stepping forward, he then called for silence, and with his voice raised above the noisy crowd, invited volunteers: two strong men were needed.

In a trice, Bradby was on his feet. He had been sitting at the front in a cap pulled low, seemingly enjoying the show along with everyone else. Watching from the wings, Sam ran his eyes over the crowd, hoping no-one would beat him to it.

'I'll volunteer!' Bradby shouted. 'I can lift a horse and cart, me!'

'Thank you, sir!' Albert boomed, throwing out a hand to invite him to step up. The crowd laughed at his claim, and a few men jeered. Meanwhile several others had risen to their feet, and after a quick survey The Great Albertini chose one: a thick-set, grinning fellow who looked reasonably sober. Soon both volunteers stood on the stage while the conjuror gave his instructions, Mirabel standing by with a lacquered casket which held the magic walnut. They duly inspected the interior of the wooden chest, which was tilted to show the audience it was empty. Then, when a snare-drum roll from the orchestra-pit had brought suspense and silence, the two lifters bent down and raised the chest easily, holding it at face height until the conjuror signalled to them to lower it.

'My friends!' The Great Albertini took a step downstage, surveying his audience with a severe look. 'You are not deceived – how could you be? It's but a wooden box, light enough to be picked up, as these good gentlemen have shown. But what, you may ask, would render such an action difficult, if not impossible?' He paused dramatically. 'Lead weights, perhaps? A load of cast iron? No, my friends, none of these. Behold – the magic walnut!'

He turned, as Mirabel stepped forward and opened the casket. As she produced the inoffensive-looking nut, she maintained an air of due solemnity; watching closely from his vantage-point, Sam nodded in silent approval. Thereafter, it was a matter of routine as Albert extolled the properties of the walnut – its mysterious origins, its uncanny power to assume the weight of a whole tree. Finally, having held it in his palm for a moment with bowed head, he placed it inside the chest and closed the lid.

'Gentlemen!' He faced the volunteers. Bradby remained blank-faced – but the other man, who was perhaps not quite as sober as Albert had judged, was grinning from ear to ear, as he had been for most of his time on stage.

'Aye aye, sir!' He called, with a clumsy attempt at a salute. 'What's your order?'

'Why – merely to do as you did before!' Albert replied loudly; he was eying the man with some suspicion. 'Both of you, on my signal, lift - if you can, that is.'

The two took their places and waited - whereupon, turning with a flourish, Albert signed to Nancy to stand well clear. It had not been rehearsed, but then, touches of improvisation on his part were not unknown. Nevertheless, Sam found himself tensing...

'Ready - lift!'

The conjuror raised a hand, then dropped it sharply. Upon his order, Bradby and the other man bent, grasped the chest – and disaster struck.

While Bradby's end remained on the stage, the other man lifted his easily – so easily that he stumbled, and had to steady himself. Then, his grin disappearing, he pushed the chest towards Bradby with both hands and shouted.

'Come on, mate, lift it up! It's not heavy – what's the matter with you?'

There was a moment: his senses frozen, Sam watched from the wings. Bradby - whether his senses were frozen or not - hesitated, then spoke up.

'Get on with you!' he called to his fellow-lifter. 'My end is as heavy as lead!'

But it wasn't - and by now the truth had dawned on each member of the Albertini company: for some reason, the electro-magnet had failed.

And like a torrent, the tension broke. The crowd erupted in a chorus of catcalls, laughter and raucous booing, to the dismay of the Guvnor - and the next moment, the burly lifter threw the chest aside with a gesture of scorn. Over it went, tumbling towards the audience, the lid flying open. Out on to the boards rattled the walnut, to roll to a halt just inches from the edge of the stage. Aghast, Sam caught a glimpse of the orchestra leader, standing dumbfounded with baton in hand.

'Magic walnut, my arse!'

The volunteer, hands on hips, stared belligerently at Albert, then at Bradby. 'You wanted me to pretend, didn't you?' he jeered. 'It's no heavier than before – it's just a shoddy trick!' To compound the insult, he faced the crowd. 'It's a fake!' he bellowed. 'And I'll bet anyone a guinea that this one was in on it!'

He was pointing at Bradby, which brought more booing. And at once Sam knew what would happen – as did Albert, who started forward…

Too late.

In a second, the company's props man, driver and bodyguard had lunged at his fellow volunteer and landed a punch to his jaw that would have felled a bullock. The crack, that could be clearly heard, produced not a gasp, but a cheer… and at once, chaos reigned.

Firstly, Bradby's victim was not felled at all: he staggered back, recovered himself, then with a roar threw himself at his assailant. Immediately the two of them were locked in a tussle, staggering about the stage and swinging punches. Nancy, quick to react, stepped back and turned to Albert, who appeared rooted with horror. Two stagehands then appeared from the wings and hurried to the combatants, struggling to separate them while the crowd, most of them on their feet now, yelled support for one man or the other. Whereupon, not knowing what else to do, the orchestra leader waved his baton and shouted to his players, who launched into some lively, stage-clearing music.

Gathering his wits, Sam strode on to the stage. Leaving the Daisy-Cup men to their task, he took Nancy's arm and sent her to the wings, telling her to go the dressing-room and lock the door. Then he turned to Albert, who appeared to be in a daze. But when Sam seized his shoulder, he turned swiftly.

'The walnut!' He cried. 'Retrieve it, for pity's sake!'

'To hell with the walnut,' Sam said under his breath. 'Get off the stage.'

'The chest, then… we must save it!'

'Later,' Sam breathed. And without further delay he half-shoved, half-dragged his father into the wings and to safety. Backstage there was confusion, more stagehands arriving to break up the brawl – for a brawl it had become. Looking back in dismay, Sam saw that at least a dozen men had clambered on to the stage and were fighting like tigers, falling over one another in clumsy abandon. Somewhere in the middle was Bradby, who had finally put his opponent out of action - only to find himself under attack from the man's friends. Cries and curses filled the air… and through it all, the orchestra played frantically on.

But in Sam's mind, as he ushered Albert up the stairs to the dressing-room, one thought rose above all others.

Someone had sabotaged the Heavy-and-Light trick, as they had almost succeeded in sabotaging the mind-reading trick at the Tivoli. And perhaps his father was right: only one man would have the desire - not to mention the audacity - to ruin The Great Albertini's act like this:

Lysander Hobbs.

***

Late that night, the exhausted and deflated Albertini company finally returned to Highgate where, with barely a word to the others, Nancy retired. The men gathered in the parlour as Sam poured out generous tumblers of whiskey. Whereupon Albert slumped down in his favourite armchair, eyes lowered.

'Lord above, Bradby.' Still on his feet, Sam gazed at the props man. 'Why did you have to lay into that loud-mouth?'

Bradby gave no answer. He was a sorry sight: bruised and battered, one jacket sleeve almost torn off, his shirt spattered with blood. Yet he remained defiant, meeting Sam's gaze without flinching: an old soldier to the last.

'He only tried to defend me – as a loyal employee should.'

Albert spoke up quietly. To Sam's relief he was recovering, though still shaken. How a fairly routine performance had turned into such a catastrophe, and at such speed, was both troubling and humiliating – but it had happened, and somehow they must deal with it.

'It was outright sabotage – do you doubt me now?' Albert's voice rose as he spoke, gazing at Sam. 'Did you believe that stagehand's tale, about a loose cable? The foot-switch was disconnected from the magnet – I'd swear it!'

Neither of the others were inclined to argue. The angry exchange with the Daisy-Cup's manager and stage manager, that had followed the riot, was yet fresh in their minds. It had taken half an hour to clear the building, assisted by the arrival of three policemen. Only then could a conversation take place, with harsh words and threats from the Hall's fast-talking manager, who was soon demanding compensation. None of his staff were remiss, he insisted: the magnet had been guarded - and if anything had gone wrong with the mechanism, then it was the fault of Albertini's man. This in turn had prompted a riposte from a breathless Bradby, who swore that the device was in good working order when he'd last seen it. The stagehand in question, however, swore that no-one had touched the magnet, and he resented the accusation, and perhaps Bradby would like to step outside and accuse him to his face… whereupon Sam, in full peacemaker mode, had finally managed to restore calm. Money changed hands, assurances were given, and the police were informed that no charges would be brought by the Daisy-Cup. So at last the company were left to gather their properties, including the Heavy-and-Light chest which was now in need of serious repair, and leave the Hall in what felt uncomfortably like disgrace.

The magic walnut, meanwhile, had vanished and was never found.

'Well then – suppose you're right. What now?'

In the parlour Sam's voice broke the silence, causing the other two to turn to him.

'Let's say that it's a matter of sabotage,' he went on. 'Moreover, let's say we've got a fair idea who might be behind it. How on earth could we prove it?'

Albert merely frowned to himself, while Sam sat down heavily and took a drink - whereupon Bradby startled both of them by banging a hand down on the arm of his chair.

'Jesus, now I recall him!' And when the other two turned, he added: 'That bald-headed devil with the toy snake – at the Tivoli!'

'I thought we were talking about tonight's foul-up, not last week's,' Sam said wryly. 'Have you had a nasty bump on the head? Besides, what does it matter now-'

'I knew I'd seen him somewhere!' Bradby insisted. 'Now it's come to me – you said you knew him too, Guvnor. Remember?'

He was regarding Albert, who nodded. 'I did, though I haven't been able to place him.'

'But I have,' Bradby said. 'He used to work at Gatti's, behind the bar. If I recall right, he got sacked for fiddling the takings…' he looked sharply at Sam. 'Do you see what I'm saying? Supposing he was paid by Hobbs?'

'I don't know,' Sam said, after a moment. 'But it would be interesting to find out.'

'Good God…' Albert sighed, and shook his head. 'At one time it wouldn't have crossed my mind that I was a big enough threat to Lysander Hobbs. When he was packing them in, and we were playing third-rate Halls… now, if he's determined to put me out of business, I suppose I should be flattered.'

'There are other conjurors, though,' Sam said, thinking fast. 'Some just as hungry. We know Hobbs is busy with his agency… might someone else be willing to pay for spoilers?' But when the other two merely eyed him, he lowered his gaze. 'I admit it's unlikely.'

'Remember the gallery-boys,' Bradby said then. Wincing a little, he was pulling off his torn jacket, examining his battle wounds. When the Vaseys turned to him, he gave a shrug.

'That's the surest and quickest way to spoil someone's act, isn't it? Pay some roughs to boo and shout, so no-one can hear what's going on onstage. Or even provoke a riot.'

It was true. Albert sighed again - but Sam raised objection.

'That isn't Hobbs' style,' he said. 'Too obvious - and too easily traced back to him. I suspect his plan – if he has one – would be simply to arrange for a few tricks to go wrong, and spread rumours that The Great Albertini's losing his touch.' He frowned. 'We must nip it in the bud – and quickly.'

'We must,' Albert said, with something of his old confidence. 'But if I know that blasted showman, he'll deny everything – he'll say I'm losing my mind. Nor is it simply a matter of money…' he paused, then: 'He wants to see me off, once and for all. Then he can rule the roost as he once did - him and Jean Balatin. A couple of villains, down to their very bones. Believe me, I know.'

To that, neither Sam nor Bradby spoke. It was rare for Albert to mention his one-time master, the brilliant but cold-hearted Frenchman who had thrilled audiences from Paris to London and beyond. Balatin had been dead for years, but would never be forgotten.

'Guvnor?' For the first time, Bradby's tiredness showed. 'If you don't mind, I'll go and get myself cleaned up and turn in. I could do with a kip...'

'Of course.' Sam drained his glass and stood up. 'Take tomorrow morning off. And get yourself a new suit – we'll pay, won't be?'

The question was directed at Albert, who nodded and raised himself stiffly. 'Take the whole day off, if you like,' he said wearily. 'I've a feeling tomorrow's show could end up being cancelled, as tonight's was originally…' he gave a sigh.'Now I think on it, I wish it had stayed cancelled, and we hadn't taken up the Daisy-Cup's offer. 'The matter was, I-'

'The matter was, you were pleased enough about it, earlier today,' Sam broke in. 'But none of us are to blame for what's happened – not even Bradby. If the man who's behind it all is who we think it is, we'll just have to find a way to stop him.'

'Yes… yes, damn it!' Albert lifted his head and took a breath. 'And I see one way - and one way only - to thwart that blasted rogue: confront him, and dare him to deny it. Go straight on the attack, and damn the consequences! So, what do you say?'

He gazed fiercely at the other two… who exchanged looks, and began to relax.

Here was The Great Albertini again: master of magic, undefeated star of the Halls, a headliner who had faced disaster before and conquered it. And if his old rival had taken it upon himself to try and knock him from his perch, he would face that challenge too.

Sam eyed Bradby, and saw him struggling to hide a lop-sided grin.

EIGHT

Lysander Hobbs occupied a comfortable set of offices off the Marylebone Road, a short distance from Madame Tussaud's waxworks. He had come a long way from the back streets of Manchester, and seldom failed to let people know it. Whereas Albert was privately ashamed of his humble roots, Hobbs was eager to remind people of his rise to fame, and to boast of his success. When The Great Albertini arrived on that cloudy Thursday morning with his manager, he was treated with courtesy and shown into Hobbs' well-furnished rooms by a smartly-dressed young clerk. As they entered the office, the man stood aside.

'Mr Hobbs is busy at present, sirs,' he said loftily. 'Please make yourselves comfortable, and he'll see you as soon as he's free.'

'What a rogue,' Albert muttered, as the clerk withdrew. 'He's putting me in my place – quite deliberate.'

'He doesn't know we're coming,' Sam objected, to which Albert merely snorted.

'I'll wager he does – he has eyes everywhere.'

'Father…' Sam gave a sigh. 'Aren't you letting your feelings about Hobbs get the better of you? We need clear heads for this meeting.'

'You think I don't know that?' Albert retorted. But while Sam took a chair in front of Hobbs' imposing desk with its shiny new telephone, the Guvnor remained on his feet, pacing about the room. He peered at portraits and framed photographs, some of them of artistes he knew. There was even one of Balatin, in top hat and tail coat, twirling his moustache like a pantomime villain – then he stopped in his tracks.

'Good God, look at this!'

Sam turned to see his father pointing at a photograph - of Albert himself. It was one of a set they had once ordered, showing The Great Albertini standing beside the Enchanted Cabinet, in dignified pose. The words *Master of Magic* were emblazoned in red letters across the top of the picture. Albert was about to comment, when abruptly the door opened and a bulky figure appeared, filling the entrance.

'Albert, old man! Admiring yourself as usual, eh? Sincere apologies for making you wait!'

The Guvnor froze, then turned with studied slowness to face his old rival, as Sam rose from his chair. The three men eyed each other: the Vaseys watchful, the other beaming with confidence. Smartly dressed as always, Hobbs came forward with hand outstretched – first to Sam, who took it and found himself gripped with more force than was necessary. Letting go, Hobbs strode towards Albert – who took the man's hand automatically, then seemed to regret it. But it was dropped at once, the other moving behind his desk to a side-table on which stood several glass decanters.

'Sherry?' He enquired. 'I have a fine Oloroso… will you join me?'

'I think not,' Albert said. But when Hobbs, still smiling, gestured him to a chair, he sat down beside Sam. With a polite but dismissive gesture, Sam also refused a drink. Whereupon Hobbs merely nodded and took his seat. Resting his elbows on a fine-tooled leather blotter, he surveyed the two of them, then:

'Have you come to talk about the Tivoli trouble? A shocking business… dreadful.'

If Albert was taken aback, he refused to show it. Sam kept expression from his own face while taking a moment to look over their host. Hobbs, a large man with a famously large appetite, looked even heavier than when he had last seen him: fleshier of face, his shock of dark hair greying at the temples. His frog-like mouth still formed a smile, that almost appeared fixed.

'Not the Tivoli,' Albert said, finding his voice. 'Though you'll know as well as we do about the tragedy… two tragedies, I should say. That's a matter for the police, however. My concerns are a lot closer to home.'

'Perhaps you've heard rumours about one or two unfortunate incidents that have occurred on our own doorstep, so to speak,' Sam said. 'May I explain?'

Hobbs raised an eyebrow. 'I think you should - Sam,' he said. 'Are you in difficulties?' He faced Albert. 'Please speak freely – we're old friends and fellow-magicians, are we not? We go back a long way.'

'Too long, Lysander.' Albert was controlling himself with an effort. 'And you won't fool a fellow-magician with that innocent air. Nor are we friends – and never have been.' And he would have said more had not the telephone chosen that moment to ring, startling him.

'Excuse me, won't you?' Hobbs said pleasantly. With a practised air he unhooked the earpiece, announced himself and listened. After a few moments, with a flickering glance at Albert, he gave a chuckle. 'I understand… we'll speak of it later. I have a small matter to deal with first… is that acceptable? Very good.'

He replaced the instrument, then looked up. 'I beg pardon – you were saying?'

'You'll excuse my father,' Sam said, somewhat shortly. 'You know he's a man of temperament. The incidents I referred to – without going into details – concern what looks like a series of attempts to sabotage our recent performances. Do you say you've heard nothing about it? Because I'd find that hard to believe.'

Hobbs met his eye. 'You would? What precisely do you mean?'

'He means someone spiked the act!'

In an instant, Albert's self-control was gone. Raising a hand, he pointed at Hobbs, whose grin was fading. 'And I can think of very few men who would dare do that – and who lack the scruples! We're here to get at the truth, Lysander. We know each other too well, you and I, so you can drop the bonhomie. Admit you had a hand in it, then we'll talk turkey – that's what you want, isn't it?'

The silence that fell then was icy. Sam half-turned to his father, willing him to keep quiet. For a moment he thought he had succeeded, until Albert looked about to unleash a tirade – but he was thwarted.

'By Christ, you've never learned a damned thing, have you?'

Hobbs's smile had vanished, to be replaced by a very hard look indeed. The mask was gone – indeed, the gloves were off too, and in one way Sam was relieved. *Go straight on the attack and damn the consequences*, the Guvnor had said the night before… he sighed. If battle was joined, then they had better face it.

'Still a hothead from Hoxton, underneath it all,' Hobbs went on, his loose mouth forming a sneer. 'For all your airs and graces - your son with his education, your big house and your carriage – but you're a scrambler, Albert. Dragged yourself up from nothing, as I did. But I don't try to hide it, and never have!' He was breathing hard now. 'And yet, we're not young lads any more… we don't go outside and settle it with our fists, as we would have done then. So state your business – get it off your chest. Then I'll have my man show you out.'

Another silence fell, of a rather different nature. Sam, angered not only by Hobbs but by his father for his reckless outburst, sought for the words. Perhaps, in a way, it would be better if they did get up and raise their fists, he thought vaguely… but Albert remained seated, glaring daggers at his arch-rival, who was unmoved.

'Well?' It was Hobbs who broke the silence. 'I'm a busy man nowadays, Albert, so I'd be obliged if you'd get to the point. Is that why you came – to accuse me of spiking your act, as you put it? Well – to be frank, I did hear what happened at the Daisy-Cup last night. But how in God's name you could think I had anything to do with it is beyond me. You rely on electrics, you court trouble - I've always said so. Unreliable… like your man Durrell, I'd guess. That dull-witted old soldier - more than likely he messed things up, and no-one else.'

With an effort, Sam kept his composure. He was stung – not so much by the man's words as by his tone of contempt, as well as his insult to Bradby. Beside him he felt his father's rage, and feared the worst. To forestall it, he gave a cough and, for effect, slapped a hand down upon the elegant desk.

'That's enough, Mr Hobbs,' he snapped. 'As it happens, we're not only talking about the Daisy-Cup. I'm thinking of last Saturday at the Tivoli, when a man came up and almost wrecked

Albert's mind-reading show. He had Paid Stooge written all over him – and he was mighty quick to take himself off when our assistant got the better of him. But we've remembered him - and so will you, I'm sure. He was sacked from Gatti's for some dirty work – likely he's not fussy how he earns his money now. Do you follow me?'

'Well, young Sam - perhaps I do,' Hobbs replied, after a pause. 'And if I'm honest, I'm a little disappointed to see you've inherited your old man's suspicious nature.' His voice had dropped to a low growl. 'You've got some nerve,' he added, eying Albert. 'Coming here, accusing me like this-'

'We assumed it was just business,' Sam broke in. 'That's your forte nowadays, isn't it? I hear you prefer sitting in your office to performing – or am I mistaken? Do you merely want to damage my father's reputation, so you can be top dog again?'

'I think he does,' Albert said, meeting Hobbs's gaze. 'It's always been a sore point, hasn't it, Lysander? Ever since I started pulling in bigger crowds than you?'

'Business, you say?' Quite suddenly, Hobbs was on his feet. He was as angry as Albert, though he controlled it better. 'By God, you've got a mighty low opinion of me, my lad.' He glared at Sam. 'You think I'd stoop to low tricks like messing up that mind-reading act? I never saw the merit of it anyway – it was bound to be rumbled sooner or later. As for paying stooges – I've no bloody need!'

He raised a hand and pointed at Albert.'I can buy you out whenever I choose, old man,' he added harshly. 'If you weren't so damned stubborn – and old-fashioned too – you'd have abandoned tricks like that years ago. I've got younger conjurors on my books now – one I brought back from the USA, would make you look like an amateur! He's the future – and you're the past. So you can take your accusations and put them somewhere dark and unpleasant. Now get out of here, and let me do some work!'

With that, he strode round the desk to the door and threw it open. At once the young clerk appeared, eyebrows raised.

'Show these men out,' Hobbs ordered. 'And keep your eyes peeled, make sure they don't lift anything as they go.'

In the silence that followed, Albert got slowly to his feet. Sam followed, breathing hard. For a moment they both eyed Hobbs, but it was clear that the visit had been a waste of time – and of energy too. Not a word was said as they moved to the door and were escorted outside. As they gained the hallway, Hobbs slammed his office door behind them.

They left the building without speaking, stepping out into the busy street. Sam was about to suggest a restorative drink: Albert looked quite shaken. Whereupon a figure appeared abruptly, startling them both.

'Mr Vasey! What a surprise – or is it?'

Standing before them was Paulo Brunner. With Hobbs's parting words still ringing in his head, Albert at first failed to recognise him. Sam, however, frowned at once.

'Paulo? What are you…?' He began – then it dawned. 'You're here to see Hobbs.'

'See him?' Paulo grinned broadly. No longer, it seemed, was he the grief-stricken son of the murdered juggler: he was the handsome, cocksure young fellow he had always been. 'I work for him now - didn't you know?' And when Sam looked blank, he added: 'One has to move on. My father…' he paused. 'My father, God rest his soul, never saw the sense of joining an agency, no matter how hard I tried to persuade him. Hobbs could have doubled his money - so I…' he shrugged. 'Well, to cut it short, when I ran into him a while back we talked, and here I am! He could use my contacts, he said, and my personality of course. So…'

But there, the young man faltered: far from looking interested in his new status or his change of luck, both Vaseys were eying him with a mixture of hostility and disbelief. Uneasily, Paulo tipped his hat as if about to move indoors – until Sam caught his arm.

'What did you mean when you said *what a surprise - or is it*?' He asked.

'Well, of course I…' Paulo looked down at his arm, but Sam held on to it.

'I naturally assumed,' he went on, raising his voice, 'that you were doing business with Mr Hobbs. A lot of acts are joining his agency – surely you know that? It makes complete sense – he's had success in America, as I recall you once did, sir…' this with a quick glance at Albert. 'New York beckons… as Mr Hobbs says, they know how to make money, do the Yanks.' He drew a quick breath, then: 'Now, much as I'd like to chat, I must be off…'

Again he looked down, whereupon Sam let go of him. Thoughts rose in quick succession, so that he barely heard Paulo's hurried goodbye before the young man disappeared. But when he turned to his father, he saw that Albert was wearing a thin smile.

'So Hobbs has hired that weasel,' he said quietly. 'As he's hired Cuddy Carter, and maybe even that rogue with the snake who was thrown out of Gatti's. What a collection, eh?' He eyed Sam grimly. 'I'll bet my life, that air of outraged innocence Hobbs put on was just another act. I still say he's out to ruin me – and I know why. He wants to see me so desperate that I'll come crawling to him, begging him to take me on as a client. Then he can make the bookings and call the shots – and take his fee. The blasted skate… we should have brought Bradby along, had him knock the fellow out cold!'

Without a word, Sam turned away to look for a cab. Behind him, he heard Albert mutter that the least that young flash-pants Paulo could have done was repay the loan he was given.

***

That afternoon, when the Vasey house was quiet, there were two telephone calls.

The first was from Sergeant Drewe. He and Sam spoke for a few minutes, but there was little to exchange: the police, it seemed, were no nearer to making an arrest for either the Carl Brunner murder or those of Chen-Li and Harold Holcombe. Sam spoke briefly of recent events, but his mind was elsewhere. Having promised once again to pass on anything of value, he rang off, thinking of tonight's show at the Oxford Music Hall in the West End. That, however, turned out to be an unfortunate premonition: the second call was from the manager of the Oxford – and as the Bedford and the Paragon had done, he was cancelling.

'Word's getting round, then. I should have expected it.'

Albert sat gloomily in the outhouse, where he had been running through a few tricks with Nancy. Receiving the news from Sam had only deepened his low mood. 'But if The Star cancels for tomorrow night…' he waved a hand dismissively. 'Then we're in real-'

'They won't.' Nancy spoke up with some impatience. 'The Oxford is never short of headliners – The Star can't afford to lose you at short notice. I said it before - the East End will keep us going.'

'She's right,' Sam said briskly. 'And they haven't seen the Enchanted Cabinet for a good while. Now that the Heavy-and-Light chest is off the bill for the present, we'll disappear Mirabel… they'll love it.'

Albert sighed, but seemed in agreement. Getting to his feet, he was about to speak when there was a knock on the door. Sam opened it, to admit Alice.

'You'd better come into the house – both of you,' she said, in a taut voice. And when the others showed surprise, she opened her hands in exasperation. 'Someone will have to deal with her, Mr Albert,' she added. 'I mean the juggler's widow – for I don't mind admitting, I'm near the end of my tether with her. Do you hear me?'

A few minutes later, with Alice having been despatched to make tea, Sam and Albert sat in the lounge facing Louise Chen.

She was unchanged, as she had been since first entering their house: veiled and composed, a forbidding presence in black. At Albert's request Nancy was also there; somehow, he thought that having another woman to hand might help. But in that, he was to be disappointed.

Madame Chen, it transpired, was now suspicious of everyone - including the very people who had given her refuge. But at least, she was willing to say a few words.

'I know I am a trial to you,' she said, her eyes on Sam. 'You need not pretend… a foreigner, and one in a plight. You wish me gone – why would you not?'

'That's nonsense,' Albert said sharply. 'I thought I made it clear that you could stay here for as long as you wish. Or at least, until you can make arrangements to travel, perhaps-'

'There's no hurry for that either,' Sam put in. 'Although, if you persist in telling us nothing – I mean about whom it is you're so afraid of, we really can't help you much.'

To that, the lady made no reply.

'Could it be you'd speak to me, Mrs Chen?' Nancy said. 'Sometimes it's awkward, isn't it? What with all that's happened, and you not having a friend to talk to, apart from Mattie…'

But she broke off - for at mention of the name their guest shook her head. 'I'm afraid to trust even Miss Burns,' she replied. 'She knew our address – my old address, I mean…' to the alarm of the others, she began working her hands together nervously. 'They are looking, even as we sit here,' she added, speaking so low that she was barely heard. 'They will not stop…'

'Who is looking?' Albert demanded, his patience evaporating. 'If only you'd tell us – and the police too – we could move matters on. Scotland Yard are desperate to make an arrest, calm public fears… you're being foolish as well as selfish, madam! Do you not see?'

A moment of silence followed. Instead of reproaching his father, Sam said nothing; he even hoped that the outburst might shake the woman into making some explanation. Nancy too kept quiet – then without warning, Louise Chen sprang to her feet.

'Foolish?' she echoed angrily. 'Do you truly think so? But then, you have no knowledge of those you speak of, sir – how could you? The ones who killed my husband will never leave London until they have killed me too! It is you who do not see!'

'Because you were a witness to the shooting, and could identify them – we know that,' Sam said. 'And so - if you know who these men are, why in heaven's name won't you say? I think you owe us some sort of explanation, don't you?'

But it was fruitless. With a sigh Louise Chen lowered her eyes, and the fire left her: once again she was the silent, unhappy figure who had appeared on the doorstep two days before. Without further word, she walked to the door and left the room.

A moment later Alice appeared with the tray. ‘Three for tea instead of four, then, is it?’ She enquired. ‘I had a feeling it might be.’

NINE

The next day, Friday, the Albertini company gathered in the outhouse to talk about the evening show at The Star in Bermondsey. To everyone's relief there had been no cancellation, and Albert was in a restless but determined mood. There and then, he announced that he was reviving The Disappearing Ape Trick.

His response was a stifled groan from Bradby, and another from Sam. Nancy, sitting on a packing case, gave no reaction.

'Are you sure about that?' Sam asked. 'Isn't making Mirabel disappear enough? Besides, it's old stuff - more trouble than it's worth.'

'Nonsense,' Albert retorted. 'And I've never done the Ape Trick at the Star. We'll dramatize it a bit, scare them to death.'

'I don't know if we still have the ape suit, Guvnor.'

Bradby, still sporting bruises from the recent melee, was looking doubtful. 'It got a bit moth-eaten, as I recall… I stored it away somewhere, but I can't recall where-'

'Don't try it on with me.' Albert wore his disapproving look. 'You know where it is, and a good shake and a brush-down will make it ready - plus a dab of black paint if necessary. It'll go down well at The Star. We just need someone to put on the suit.' He looked pointedly at Sam, who quickly shook his head.

'Not me,' he said firmly. 'My days of playing the ape are long over. Besides…' he threw a meaningful glance at Bradby, 'I wouldn't fit into that suit now, would I?'

'That's true,' Bradby replied, straight-faced. 'Mr Sam's not the spindly lad he was – I mean it in a complimentary way, of course.' To Albert, he said: 'If you're set on this, we'd need to hire a stooge - and quick.'

'As it happens, I know someone,' Nancy said, after a pause. And when the others turned, she added: 'An old friend… been on stage before. I'll tell him what to do, and you can run it over with him before we go on. He's a quick learner.'

'Indeed?' Albert looked suspicious. 'Where has this fellow

sprung from?'

'Ask no questions and I'll tell no lies, Alby,' she replied. 'Don't you trust me?'

'You know he does,' Sam said. 'And if he's set on it…' he glanced at Albert. 'Then we'll just have to trust his judgement too, won't we?'

But of course, the matter was already settled; the Guvnor's word was law, and if a temporary assistant needed to be brought in, so be it.

***

The young man hired to wear the ape suit – a gorilla-like costume with thick black fur, and a realistic-looking mask – was called Arthur. He arrived at The Star in Bermondsey with Nancy, who brought him backstage. The show had already begun, a troupe of acrobats working hard while the hall filled up. Coates, the wiry little stage manager, seemed in good spirits – and highly relieved that there was no need for the electro-magnet this time. In The Great Albertini's dressing room, however, the atmosphere was somewhat tense.

'Are you sure you know what to do? I mean, to the last detail?' The Guvnor, having drilled Arthur as to his part in the illusion, was on edge. Sam, however, was satisfied: the young man seemed eager to please. He had never had a chance like this before, he said. It was an honour to appear with the great conjuror – he would rather die than let him down.

'Don't you worry about a thing, sir,' he assured Albert, nodding vigorously. He had already donned the costume, though not the furry head with the mask. 'If you can get a couple of stagehands to lead me on, I'll scare the britches off everyone.' For good measure he beat his chest and let out a roar that filled the room.

'Yes, yes…' Albert winced. 'Just be sure you go quiet once the curtain's drawn, and wait for Nancy's cue.'

'And don't rattle the bars too hard,' Bradby added, from his perch on a props case. 'They're only wooden poles, painted to look like iron – I had to fit them in a tearing hurry.'

He threw a look at Albert, but was ignored. Nancy, already in her Mirabel costume, was looking at Arthur. There was a moment, in which Sam caught a private glance pass between the two of them. Precisely what relations were between Nancy and her so-called friend he did not know. She hadn't spoken of a new beau, but…

A loud knock on the door startled everyone. When Sam went to unbolt it and draw it open, however, he broke into a smile. Standing aside, he announced Miss Florence Bates.

'I saw you were on the bill too – just had to come and wish you well,' Florrie proclaimed, striding in dressed in her male attire and swinging her famous, antique walking cane. Bradby got to his feet with a foolish grin, which caused Sam to stifle a laugh. Albert managed a smile too; he usually discouraged visitors, but Florrie was special.

'My dear, how are you?' He cried. 'Elegant as always… it's we who should wish you well. Are you on next?'

'Next but one,' Florrie said. 'I like to follow a *chanteuse* – that's what the woman calls herself, anyway. A female singer, I mean… it makes a contrast, see.' She drew a monocle from her top pocket, screwed it in place and surveyed them all with a haughty look. At that, even Albert gave a chuckle. Nancy, however, seemed unmoved.

'Well now, who's this?' Florrie's eyes had fallen on Arthur, who dropped his gaze in apparent embarrassment. 'No need to be afraid, young sir – I won't eat you.'

'He's just helping us out,' Albert said, somewhat quickly. No-one else was supposed to draw attention when The Great Albertini was present.

With her usual tact Florrie raised her top hat to him, smiled at everyone again and said she would leave them to get ready. Sam saw her out to the passage, where she turned to him. 'I see Albert's revived the Ape Trick,' she said. 'I hope it goes down a storm.' She smiled briefly. 'Well, we must soldier on… whatever happens, eh?'

And she was gone, twirling her cane as she strode down the corridor. Thoughtfully Sam went back inside the dressing-room, closed the door – and gave a start.

In his absence, Arthur had put on the ape's head and was crouching before him, swinging his arms. Watched by all, he uttered a growl and beat his chest rapidly, rotating his body from side to side.

He would do, Sam thought; and even Albert gave a grudging nod of approval.

***

When the Act went as well as it did this night, it was a joy – nothing less.

Memories of Sam's recent troubles had faded, for a time at least. Standing in the wings as usual, watching Albert at his most assured with a good crowd present, he felt a happiness that was rare nowadays. Most of his life was work and worry: dealing with hard-nosed managers and impresarios, paying bills and chasing payments. But occasions such as this made it all worthwhile, and he intended to savour it. Tonight, from Albert's entrance to loud applause and cheers, the Star's audience had lapped up every trick, every well-turned phrase. Even the backstage men were enjoying the show, some watching from the opposite wing. Soon Coates appeared at his side, wearing a toothy smile.

'Glee… that's what I'm feeling right now, Mr Vasey,' he murmured. 'Sheer glee, and a full house too. I can't wait to see the gorilla trick – all set, is it?'

'Any minute now,' Sam told him.

He was right, for the moment had arrived. While The Great Albertini addressed the audience, stagehands wheeled on the Enchanted Cabinet, hastily adapted by Bradby to house the captive gorilla. Now there was a different door on the front: a frame of vertical bars to make it into a cage, with a red velvet curtain for the conjuror to draw across. Otherwise, it appeared empty as it always did. What nobody knew, apart from a few other illusionists, was that the inside of the cabinet was lined with two hinged, floor-to-ceiling mirrors, their backs painted the same pattern as the walls. Once the person who would disappear - usually Mirabel - was inside the cabinet and hidden from view, she would flatten herself against its back and draw the mirrors towards her so that they formed a closed triangle of ninety degrees – but because they were mirrors, they reflected the cabinet walls to the audience, making it appear empty. It never failed, so long as everyone knew what they were doing.

The other thing nobody knew, was that Nancy was already inside the cabinet.

During Albert's previous trick, the audience was so intrigued that they had barely noticed her leaving the stage. Once in the wings her task was to enter the cabinet, pull the mirror-doors towards her and vanish. When it was brought on-stage, Arthur in his ape suit had gone inside and the curtain were drawn, the two of them would simply change places so that the ape turned into Mirabel. After she was shown, and Albert had convinced the crowd that the ape had disappeared, they would repeat the procedure in reverse – Mirabel would turn back into the ape.

'My friends!' The Great Albertini surveyed his audience with great solemnity. 'To-night is a very special night! And where better, I ask, to show this stupendous, even dangerous procedure, than here at The Star? Are you ready to be amazed, by The Disappearing Ape?'

Before the crowd could voice approval, he turned dramatically towards the wing opposite Sam's and clapped his hands. The orchestra played a flourish - and Arthur was on.

Led by two stagehands, struggling and straining against the rope they held, he faced the audience and roared, causing a mixture of alarm and delight. People laughed and roared back, which only enraged the ape further. He beat his chest and lunged at the stagehands, who played their parts well, forcing him to the cabinet. Once he was inside and the cage door was fastened, Arthur gripped the bars and growled, directing his fury at The Great Albertini – but when the conjuror raised a hand and pointed, he went quiet.

'Do not be afraid!' Albert ordered, turning to the crowd. 'The creature is safely confined, as he has been since he was brought to me from darkest Africa! Moreover, he is now in my power! Observe with your own eyes the magic of the ancients – witness the transformation!'

He glanced down to the orchestra pit, and a drum-roll began. While the drummer played, the great illusionist moved to the cabinet and drew the curtain across with a dramatic flourish, concealing the crouching ape. He then bowed his head in concentration, while the audience went quiet. When the drummer finally stopped, there was silence.

'Hear that?' Coates whispered to Sam. 'You could hear a pin drop!'

'Behold – it is accomplished!' Albert's voice filled the auditorium. Raising a hand, he turned and pulled the curtain back… to reveal an empty cabinet.

Sam stared, and his heart gave a jolt. Where was Nancy? Beside him, Coates looked puzzled.

'Isn't your girl supposed to do a swap with the gorilla?' He asked, under his breath. Sam made no reply, but looked hard at Albert: somehow, he must manage the situation.

'Gone, my friends – passed into another sphere!'

Standing stiff as a board, Albert gestured to the cabinet, willing the crowd to follow him. At least the ape had vanished, as promised… swiftly he seized the box and turned it about on its castors, as he always did.

'No trapdoors, no sliding panel, my friends – The Great Albertini scorns such feeble devices, as used by lesser magicians!' He cried. 'But where is the ape, you ask – is he truly banished to some other realm? What do you say?'

He was playing for time, and Sam watched in hope: whatever had gone wrong, he reasoned, there was still a chance it could come right. Though how both Albert and Nancy could squeeze themselves into the tight triangle at the rear of the cabinet, he couldn't imagine…

'Come, don't hesitate to speak up!' The Great Albertini had moved downstage, encouraging the audience to call out suggestions. Obligingly, a few people did: there was a false floor, someone suggested – he's squeezed himself behind the curtain, someone else shouted. Forcing a smile, the conjuror shook his head and, moving back to the cabinet, shook the curtain aside to show that it was not so. He then bent forward slightly, and Sam guessed that under his breath he was issuing terse instructions. It was not yet a disaster, but it was close: any more of this and the act could become little more than pantomime, with people calling out at random. For The Great Albertini, such an outcome would be unthinkable.

'Enough – we will now recall him!'

Albert faced the crowd again, raising his hands for silence. Once again, he turned and drew the curtain across the barred cabinet door. Again, he bowed his head in concentration while the drummer, at a signal from his leader, began playing another roll. When he stopped, with a sharp rap on the snare drum, Albert whirled round and drew back the curtain.

As before, the cabinet was empty.

This time the reaction was ominous: first a murmur, then a muttering giving way to loud voices – and then the booing started. People shouted out scornfully, others jeered… a few men got to their feet, gesturing angrily. They felt cheated; that one of the most famous conjurors in London could fail them so dismally was an insult.

Sam was thinking fast - and one thing became clear: Nancy was not in the cabinet, and never had been. Given the cramped space, Arthur in his ape suit had to be hiding behind the mirrored panels. But worst of all, he was remaining there – which had to be deliberate.

It was sabotage again, of the most dramatic and blatant kind. Thoughts flew up: of the failure of the Heavy-and-Light chest, of the near-failure of the mind-reading trick, of their meeting with Lysander Hobbs and his flat denials – but there was no time. Drawing a deep breath, ignoring Coates who was gesturing wildly across the stage to his men, he walked out and faced the crowd.

'Ladies and gentlemen, please!' He shouted. 'If I might explain…'

But it was no use: the crowd were angry, even threatening. While Albert stood centre-stage in apparent shock, stagehands hurried on and wheeled the cabinet off into the wings. The orchestra struck up frantically, and almost at once another act appeared: a well-known tenor. Ignoring the Vaseys, spreading his arms wide, the man strode down to the footlights to seize the moment. Whereupon the orchestra leader called to his players, waved his baton wildly, and at once they launched into the singer's opening number. As the man broke into song, all Sam could do was take Albert by the arm and lead him off into the wings, where the Enchanted Cabinet stood forlornly, its barred door wide open

His pulse racing, Sam glanced inside to see that the mirrored panels had been opened, but not pushed against the walls, leaving the means of concealment visible to anyone who bothered to look.

Not that it seemed to matter, for it was as clear as daylight now that the cabinet was quite empty.

Not only had Arthur in his ape suit disappeared, but so had Nancy.

TEN

Miss Florence Bates would shed some light on the mystery - but only a little.

In stunned silence they sat in The Great Albertini's dressing-room with the door firmly bolted: Sam, Albert and Bradby. Outside, order had been restored, the well-known tenor extending his act to include a few singalong tunes that pleased the crowd. With regard to the Star's backstage men, however, it had been a different story: hostile looks and angry questions thrown at the Vaseys, that stopped short of threats only because of Albert's status. Though how long he would retain that status was now in doubt.

Also present was Florrie Bates, who had changed out of her male attire. Though looking uneasy, she had stayed to offer a little comfort

'Tell me again,' Sam said, breaking the silence. 'You spoke to her, and she told you all was well?'

'Near enough,' Florrie nodded. 'When she came off-stage, she saw me watching and said she was going out the back for a minute. But anyway, when I saw your young man in his ape suit bounding up, I clean forgot about her. He scared me stiff!'

'So she was never inside the cabinet, as you thought.' Bradby said, his eye on Sam. Sitting in a corner, the props man looked even more dismayed than did his employers.

'But… then, why would Arthur stay hidden as he did?'

For the first time since he had left the stage, Albert spoke up in a voice of bewilderment. And though Sam and Bradby shared a few suspicions, they kept quiet.

'And where did he go?' The Guvnor went on, without looking at anyone. 'He must have been inside the cabinet when they rolled it off.'

'Well, that's the oddest part,' Florrie said. And when Albert looked up, she spread her hands. 'No sooner was the box in the wings, he shot out of it like a rabbit! Still in his costume, though he'd taken the head off. The stagehands saw him too, though no-one stopped him… likely they were as startled as I was.'

'Did you see where he went?' Sam asked. In his mind, things seemed to be fitting together.

'Well, I didn't look,' Florrie said. 'To tell the truth, I was worried about the crowd. I thought bedlam would break out.'

'It did,' Albert said quietly. 'The act was ruined… I could be ruined.'

Helplessly, he looked round at those he trusted: his son and his loyal props man, either of whom would walk over hot coals for him. 'They'll all cancel, now,' he added forlornly. 'I'll be tomorrow's headline, for the worst of reasons…' his face darkening, he eyed Sam. 'Perhaps Hobbs has won, after all.'

'No, he hasn't!' Sam got determinedly to his feet. 'I won't hear of it,' he went on. 'We'll take a break, while I talk to people – we still have friends.' He glanced at Florrie. 'And the entertainment papers will give us another chance, if we come up with a story. We've been cruelly betrayed, but we've faced trouble before.' He paused, looking at his father. 'Maybe Paulo Brunner was right – you could do another American tour, let things die down here. People have short memories. Once you're back with some new tricks, you can relaunch…'

'No, Sam.' Albert met his eye, shaking his head. 'I won't run away to America - that would be a coward's move. Though I think I need a breathing space…' he gave a sigh. 'A week, perhaps two. Once we know what happened with Nancy and Arthur, it might be possible to make a statement of some sort, give an interview or two…'

He trailed off, whereupon Sam and Bradby exchanged looks. It was a setback, and a bad one, but it was not a defeat. They would rebuild… with hopes rising, Sam nodded.

'Very well,' he said. 'I'll get busy tomorrow – for now, we could all do with getting home. And our thanks go to you, Florrie.'

'We won't forget our friends, Miss Bates,' Bradby put in.

'Oh, get on!' Florrie looked embarrassed. 'The best thing you can do is find another assistant quick, and bring the act back on stage - but I wouldn't hire any more amateurs. You should have sounded that young fellow out, through and through.'

The three men merely looked at each other.

***

Sam was in the office early the following morning, with a cup of strong coffee to hand; he had barely touched his breakfast. And as he expected, the telephone was soon ringing. Tonight's show was cancelled, and the one after that. Soon he took the initiative and began interrupting callers to say that The Great Albertini was unable to appear at present, because of illness. Nothing to be alarmed about, he insisted, and the company was taking the opportunity to rebuild the act. He would be in touch just as soon as he could…

But following what must have been the sixth call, when a sour-voiced promoter told him to leave that for a while – maybe for a year or two - he gave up and disconnected the instrument. Thereafter, he sat at the desk and tried to think.

Now that he had digested it, after a night of troubled sleep, he saw a pattern that both appalled and angered him. It seemed clear enough: for reasons best known to herself Nancy had been intent on damaging Albert's act, for the past fortnight at least. First there was the alarming incident at the Tivoli, when the bald man with the toy snake had come close to ruining the mind-reading session. Sam knew that Nancy could not have seen through the blindfold – nobody could. How, then, could she have seen the snake? The fact that she had been cagey about it ever since only strengthened his suspicions. It was a near-thing, and had she not kept up the illusion by identifying the object, the trick would have been exposed. She had saved the day – but how could she have known what the volunteer was holding, unless she had foreknowledge? And could that near-disaster merely have been a warning?

But then there had been the failure of the Heavy-and-Light trick at the Daisy-Cup, which was far more serious. Sam was still unsure how the electro-magnet had become disconnected, but like his father he believed it was a matter of sabotage. On that occasion Nancy had been merely a bystander – but could he be certain she was not a party to it? And even leaving that aside, last night's catastrophe at The Star had put the lid on it. Not only had she left the Hall before the cabinet was brought on, with stagehands believing she was already concealed inside it - it was she who had introduced Arthur.

Don't you trust me?

Her question to Albert came back to him in an instant, making his mouth tighten. They had all trusted her – why should they not? The notion that she could be a *saboteuse* chilled him – was it merely a matter of money, he wondered? Could she really have been in the pay of Lysander Hobbs – and if so, since when? It had to be after Hobbs returned from America, which was not long before the near-failure of the mind-reading act…

With an effort, he shook himself: such speculation was useless now. Nor was there any use in trying to confront Hobbs again: even if he agreed to see them there would be denials – and what proof did the Vaseys have? The Great Albertini's star had fallen, and it would be a hard task to raise it again. With his father stunned by the events, Sam had to take action – and for the present he saw only one course: to go to Nancy's flat in Islington and demand an explanation – provided she was still there. On that score, he had doubts.

But it must be done. Within a short while he had left the house and taken a cab down the Holloway Road, alighting at Highbury Corner. From there it was a short walk down busy Upper Street to a side-street of terraced houses near the Agricultural Hall. He reached number eleven, glanced up at the first-floor window and saw that it was curtained, then rang the doorbell.

There was a moment, which became a half-minute, then a minute. Impatiently Sam rang again, and at last heard the noise of a bolt being drawn. The door opened a few inches, and a female head peered round - but it was not Nancy's.

'Good morning,' Sam said, removing his hat. 'I'm here to see Miss Poole – Nancy Poole. May I come in?'

The other blinked at him, but did not answer.

'Would you be her sister?' Sam enquired. 'My name's Vasey – I'm her employer. It's important that I see her without delay.'

'Sister - bloody hell, is that what she told you?'

The door opened wider, and the figure revealed herself as a woman of perhaps thirty years, blue-eyed and fair-complexioned. She was wearing a brightly-patterned silk dressing-gown – at sight of which Sam gave a start.

It was Nancy's Chinese gown.

'That's what she said - that she lived with her sister,' he replied. 'May I ask who you are?'

'You can ask,' came the reply; the woman's gaze was far from friendly. 'But I can't see it's any of your business. As for Nancy, she doesn't live here now. Up and gone.' And when Sam demanded when she had left, the other grew resentful.

'Yesterday. Now I'm going back to bed… got a cold coming on-'

'My apologies,' Sam broke in, cutting her short. 'But if you'd be good enough, I must insist on looking at Nancy's room. It's… an offence may have been committed,' he added, making it up as he spoke.

'What?' The woman flinched. 'You're not the police, are you?'

'As it happens, I've been assisting them in certain respects,' Sam told her. 'But there's no need to call them in. I won't take long, and I shouldn't need to trouble you further… miss?'

'Willens,' came the reply, after a pause. 'I'm…. I was her friend.' Suddenly she gave a start. 'Employer, is it? You mean, you're the magician – The Great Albertini?'

Sam shook his head. 'Not me, I'm just his errand-boy. Nancy might have left a few things behind that belong to us, you see. So - may I come in now?'

With a resigned look Miss Willens turned away, leaving the door ajar. Sam entered the house, closed the door and followed her up a creaking and uncarpeted stairway.

***

It was a very small flat, with just one bedroom. And quite quickly, Sam learned something new about Nancy. One glance through the open bedroom door revealed a rumpled double bed, which was enough.

'We share everything,' his host said. She was standing across the sitting room from him with her arms folded. 'We're more than sisters – her own wouldn't give her the time of day.'

Sam turned slowly to gaze at the woman - whereupon a look of defiance appeared.

'Well, she could have told us,' he said, with a sigh. 'It's not important - my father…' he paused. 'The Great Albertini is my father, and like me he judges people by their skills and by their character – not by whom they share a bed with.'

'That's mighty generous of you', Miss Willens said.

'I mean no ill-will,' Sam persisted. 'The matter is…' he thought for a moment, and decided on frankness. 'Nancy bolted last night - in the middle of the act. Left my father in the lurch, to face an angry crowd. She left the theatre – The Star in Bermondsey – and hasn't been seen since. So…' he drew a breath. 'Can you say anything that might help me understand? Because just now, things look pretty bad for us, Miss Willens. And that's the truth.'

'By Jesus – then she's really done it!' The other met his gaze, then looked away. 'I didn't think she would,' she went on. 'The sneaky little bitch…'

'What do you mean?' Sam asked sharply.

'She was earning good money from you, wasn't she?' Miss Willens frowned, seemingly piecing it out as she spoke. 'But seems it wasn't enough. I told her she was lucky, but she said she could double her wages. We could have a fine life together, she said - in France, or somewhere like that. I didn't believe her – even that day she came home a bit drunk, saying it was all settled. I asked her what was settled, but she wouldn't say.'

'I thought you said you shared everything,' Sam said, with a touch of bitterness.

'So we did,' came the reply. 'But she started meeting someone – a man, I thought. We argued then – something we hardly ever did. After that, things were never the same…'

She broke off, suddenly upset. Sam gave a nod, and changed his tone.

'You have my sympathies,' he said. 'For it looks as if she's betrayed us all.'

Miss Willens said nothing, but moved to a chair and sat down heavily.

'Can you tell me when that was?' He asked. 'The time she came home and said it was all settled?'

'About a fortnight since.'

'And she never mentioned names – or said anything about who she was meeting?'

The woman merely shook her head.

'So, you never saw her again after yesterday?'

'She left early, before I was even awake.' Nancy's ex-partner looked up. 'She must have packed a bag, took most of her things… except this.' She fingered the sleeve of the Chinese gown. 'She knew I always liked it… now it looks as if it was her parting gift.'

'How did you know she wasn't coming back?' Sam persisted. 'Did she leave a note, or…?'

'No note. But you might take a look at the dressing-table.'

With a frown he turned to the bedroom, took a step inside – and froze. On a large mirror above the cluttered dressing-table, words had been scrawled in red greasepaint:

Gone for keeps, dearest. Chin up, Nance.

Chin up… he could hear her saying it, as she had so often done. With a heavy heart he returned to the main room, where Miss Willens had risen from her chair.

'You said there might be some things of yours here,' she said in a dull voice. 'You'd better take a look around.'

'There's no need,' Sam said, preparing to leave. 'I think I've seen enough.'

'I can tell you one thing, though.'

He turned to see the woman looking thoughtful. 'When I look back a few days, I think she'd changed a bit,' she said. 'I mean, from how she was when she'd first talked about doubling her wages. She was scared, I'd say. Don't ask me what of, for I haven't a notion.'

'I thank you for that, Miss Willens,' Sam said, though the business seemed as murky as before; if anything, it was even murkier. 'Will you be all right here? Alone, I mean? If there's anything we can do for you-'

'Lord above!' The other broke in. 'What are you thinking of – to hire me as her bloody replacement?'

With a polite nod, Sam put on his hat and left.

***

He did not return to Highgate. On a whim, he took a cab down to The Strand to pay a call on Sergeant Drewe at Scotland Yard. For a while he had harboured a vague notion of reporting Nancy as a missing person, but decided against it. She was no such thing: she was a free agent, who had chosen her own path - one of greed and betrayal, he thought grimly. And yet, it might help to talk of other matters with the sergeant. Being preoccupied with the company's troubles, he had barely thought about the murders at the Tivoli… now, events came back in a rush. He was still mulling them over as he paid the cabman, and began to think of his silent and un-cooperative guest back in Highgate: Louise Chen. Pushing the thought away, he walked into the building.

Fortunately, it turned out that the sergeant was in. So too was Inspector Maskell, he was told – a man whom Sam had all but forgotten about. Adopting a business-like manner he entered the office, upon which a startled Drewe rose up from his desk.

'Mr Vasey… why, this is most opportune. The inspector was going to telephone you - this very morning. I offered to do it instead, but he… well, now you're here...'

He broke off, caught up a chair and brought it to his desk. Briefly they shook hands, and Sam sat down facing him. He was unsure how to begin, but noticing that the other man appeared ill-at-ease, he spoke up.

'I beg your pardon, sergeant, but I've been busy lately,' he began. 'You may not have heard, but we've had some difficulties with the act. Things we couldn't possibly have foreseen… but in any case, I fear I've nothing new to tell you. Have you…'

'Have I anything to tell you, sir?' Drewe finished. 'As it happens, I have…' he hesitated, looking down at his desk, at which Sam too found himself growing uneasy. 'Though I'm afraid we haven't caught our murderer - that search goes on, even more urgently.'

With eyebrows raised, Sam waited.

'And what's worse - much worse - is that he's still active, or so it appears,' the sergeant continued. 'It's… it's most troubling. I think… in fact, I think you should speak to Inspector Maskell after all. If you'll forgive me...'

Somewhat hurriedly he stood up, went to the door and threw it open, calling out to someone to fetch the inspector immediately A voice answered, whereupon Drewe returned to his seat. Sam watched him, a frown forming.

'You alarm me,' he said at last. 'I might even suspect there's been another murder – surely not?'

Then he caught his breath - and before the other answered, he knew it.

'You're quite correct, Mr Vasey,' Drewe said, meeting his eye. 'A most terrible one… of course, we cannot be certain that the same man is responsible, but given the Music Hall connection…' he took a breath. 'The inspector is most eager not to cause a panic, so I must ask for your complete discretion.' And when Sam said nothing, he added: 'The body was found just off Tower Bridge Road. Death was by means of stabbing - a powerful stroke to the heart. Again, no witnesses – and again, no apparent motive. The only clue was a man's cuff-link, apparently dropped by the assailant.'

A coldness was stealing over Sam. He was forming a question when footsteps sounded from the doorway, and he turned to see Inspector Maskell walk in. At sight of him, the man halted abruptly.

'Mr Vasey… you're here already. Please accept my deepest condolences… it's been a shock for us all - but worse for you, of course.'

Slowly, Sam got to his feet – whereupon Sergeant Drewe spoke up with some urgency. 'I haven't told him the victim's identity yet, sir,' he said, far too loudly. 'After what you said earlier, I was going to leave it to you.'

A moment passed, in which Sam felt his heart thump. He saw acute embarrassment flicker across Maskell's features, to be replaced by a look of resignation. With barely a nod at Drewe, he took a step towards Sam – who stared in dismay.

'Condolences?' He echoed.

'I meant, in view of your relations with the young woman,' the inspector replied tautly. 'Forgive me, I thought you'd been told…'

'Who is it?' Sam demanded. 'Who's been murdered, for

God's sake?'

But it was Drewe who provided the answer. Before Maskell could speak again he gave a cough, which made Sam turn swiftly. Whereupon, he heard the words as if from a distance – as if spoken in a dream.

'The murdered woman is Miss Nancy Poole,' Drewe said. 'Your employee - I should say, the former employee of your father.'

'I'm most dreadfully sorry,' he added.

But Sam barely heard him.

ELEVEN

She had been found early that morning, by a night watchman who was on his way home. Having summoned the police, the man left them to their grisly task of examining the body - but as it happened, identification was simple enough. Nancy's travelling-bag was beside her, containing clothes and other items including a purse and a small diary with her name and address. The bag had been rifled and the purse was empty, which might have suggested robbery as a motive – but Scotland Yard, and the Vaseys too, thought differently.

At Highgate, Albert was broken by the news, and sat slumped in his armchair in a dressing-gown, though it was past mid-day. Having heard the details from Sam, he was struggling to take them in. Alice had made him a hot drink laced with brandy, but he had barely touched it.

'Perhaps that inspector was right,' he murmured at last. 'Could this murderous wretch be someone from our world after all – from the Halls? Though not a rival juggler…' he sighed heavily. 'I once said that as a joke. What possessed me to be so callous?'

Sam made no reply, having returned home in turmoil. He had stopped by at Bradby's lodgings to tell him the awful news, whereupon the props man had volunteered to go to Nancy's widowed mother, whom he believed still lived in Limehouse. Following that, he would come at once to Highgate.

'And what of this other business?' Albert said suddenly, with a frown. 'The woman in the flat who isn't her sister – far from it - and turns out to have known a great deal more about Nancy's doings than we did?' He lowered his eyes, then: 'I've never held my fellow humans in very high regard, Sam… I've been in this business too long, known too many rogues. But I trusted that girl - in fact I adored her, in a way. Not as I did your mother, you understand,' he added. 'But…'

'I know, father,' Sam said.

They were silent for a while. Albert took up his drink and

sipped at it. 'I suppose I should rally myself, start looking for a new Mirabel,' he said at last. 'There's much to do – but to tell the truth, I haven't the stomach for it just now.'

Sam met his eye, and was troubled. Albert was a fighter and always had been, but Nancy's betrayal, followed by her brutal murder, had unnerved him. For the present, there was no possibility of rebuilding the act. They would have to take things a day at a time: wait for inquests, attend funerals, help the police if they could. An uncertain period stretched ahead. After a while, Alice came in to ask if there was anything they needed - but when Sam signalled there was not, she caught his eye. Making a brief excuse to his father, he followed her outside.

'Is something the matter?' He asked; Alice appeared quite agitated.

'The tele-thing rang again, while you were out – twice,' she said. 'And both times there was no-one there. I asked who it was, but they rang off. And that's not all - I swear, Mr Sam, someone was prowling around outside the house in the night. Woke me up… I came down to the kitchen, but all was as it should be. Even so, I know there was someone. And I wasn't dreaming, if that's what you think.'

'Did you try the doors and windows?' Sam asked, with a frown. 'Were they all closed and locked – could it have been the wind?'

'There was no wind to speak of. And I know the sound of footsteps when I hear them. And everything was locked and bolted – I checked like I always do.'

'Well, let me think on it, Alice,' he said, somewhat absently. 'Just now, there's-'

'Yes, I know…' she bit her lip. 'I shouldn't have bothered you, should I. I'm like a cat on hot bricks today. It's too awful…' she shook her head. 'What can I do for Mr Albert? He's had a terrible shock.'

'So long as you're willing to stay, it's enough,' Sam told her. 'He needs you,' he added, inclining his head towards the parlour door. 'Perhaps more than you think.'

But when Alice lowered her gaze and turned to go, a thought struck him.

'What of our guest?' He asked. 'Has she been down – has she spoken?'

'She took breakfast in the kitchen. But she still stays in her room…' Alice hesitated, then: 'I was talking to someone I know, out shopping. She said there are French people in Soho, might look after her better than we can. If she'll listen to advice, that is…' she sighed. 'I haven't seen much sign of that, so far.'

With that she went off to the kitchen. Sam was about to return to the parlour when he heard Bradby's voice. He had come in the back door, and was speaking with Alice. At once Sam went to join them - but at sight of him, Bradby spread his hands.

'No luck,' he said, grim-faced. 'No Mrs Poole at that address. There's another family living there, with a horde of kids… they've never heard of Nancy.'

***

For the Albertini Company, the next few days passed in something of a blur; but for Sam it was particularly gruelling.

To begin with, since no relatives could be found, he was asked by the police to formally identify Nancy's body at the mortuary. That grim business over and done, he paid a brief visit to Miss Willens and broke the news. But if he had been braced for tears, he was surprised: the woman merely thanked him and disappeared inside, banging the door behind her.

He was left in little doubt that he would not see her again.

By the following Wednesday he was restless. He had made telephone calls to friends in the Music Hall world, and heard the same shocked response from everyone. He had spoken with Sergeant Drewe, and learned that inquests on all of the murder victims had now been carried out, and delivered the expected verdict of murder by person or persons unknown. One had died of strangulation, two of gunshot wounds, the last by stabbing. The same perpetrator was suspected, but the police were pursuing various lines of enquiry. Which thus far, Sam knew, had proved fruitless.

After that, things went quiet in the Vasey home. Albert often retired to the outhouse to try out a few new tricks, or so he claimed. Though mostly, Sam knew, he merely sat by himself. The only time he had left the house was to attend Nancy's funeral, which Sam had arranged hastily at a church in Islington. Apart from the Vasey company, there were few mourners: Mattie Burns and one or two others from the Halls. Florrie Bates sent flowers and a message of condolence; Miss Willens did not attend.

That Wednesday morning, Sam decided to take a cab to the Tivoli. He had the idea of talking with Edgar Downs and John Chambers. Now that the news had broken, the whole Music Hall community was shaken – and so, to the alarm of the police, were the general public. A killer was surely abroad, as during those fateful weeks in Whitechapel, three years before – and now that a woman was the latest victim, the matter had taken on a new urgency. Dressed soberly in a dark suit and necktie, Sam arrived at the Tivoli and was admitted to the manager's office.

But what he had intended as a casual call, would turn into something quite different.

'Please accept my sincere sympathies,' Downs said, after they had shaken hands. 'It's tragic… no, it's worse. It's plain evil.'

He gestured to a chair, whereupon Sam nodded and accepted a glass of whiskey. There followed an awkward silence, while the manager sat down. Finally, he looked up.

'As it happens, there have been some surprising events here too, though of a very different nature,' he said. 'Of course, all the staff who knew Nancy have been shocked, but some have taken it particularly hard. One was young Billy Bowes – you may recall he was the one who discovered poor Carl Brunner…' Downs shook his head. 'Well, the upshot is, the lad's taken off – left without even a good-bye. Nobody seems to know why.'

Sam took in the news without expression. If Billy Bowes had been attracted to Nancy, he was far from the only one – whereupon he thought suddenly of Paulo Brunner. He had half-expected the young man to attend her funeral, but there had been no sign of him.

'I meaned to ask - how is Mr Vasey taking it?' The Tivoli's manager enquired. 'It must be appalling for him… I imagine you're pausing the act, for the time being?'

'We are,' Sam replied. 'And my father is well enough, despite the shock. We're taking time to adjust, of course. But he wants to be back on the stage as soon as it's possible. Magic is his passion – his very life-blood.'

'Of course…' Downs looked uncomfortable. 'Though as you might expect, it may be some time before we could consider re-booking… I hope you understand.'

'I do,' Sam said, and finished his drink. 'I merely wished to keep in contact… my father has always held the Tivoli in the highest regard – as he has you, Mr Downs.'

He rose to take his leave, but the other lifted a hand to stay him.

'Please don't go away with the wrong impression. I've known many performers, including a few illusionists – but your father is one of the best, and I hold him in great regard too. Once things have died down…' he sighed. 'When this murderous person is caught – and hanged too, I hope – we can begin a return to how things were. I'm determined upon it – and that includes seeing The Great Albertini back on our stage. You have my word.'

With that he stood up and held out his hand, and Sam took it. Meeting the other's eye, he discerned a kindness in the gruff manager. They parted amicably, with a slight lightening of heart on Sam's part.

On his way out he thought to pass a moment with John Chambers, but it seemed the stage manager was busy elsewhere. However, while heading for the door he ran into a man he recognised: Dan, the older stagehand who had comforted Billy Bowes on that fateful evening when Carl Brunner was killed. At sight of him, the man touched his cap and nodded.

'I know about your troubles, sir,' he said. 'I was most sorry to hear.' But when Sam murmured his thanks and began to move away, he stepped closer.

'You know Billy Bowes took off?' He peered at Sam from beneath grizzled eyebrows.

'I heard,' Sam nodded. 'Maybe it all got a bit too much for him – with Brunner's death, and then Chen-Li's, I mean. He was very shaken, as I recall.'

'He was - but not as shaken as when the news came in of your… of what happened to Mr Albert's assistant. I was there, when we got the word - Billy went as white as flour.'

'Perhaps he was sweet on her,' Sam said, his mind drifting. Not that it would have done him much good, he thought privately.

'No, sir - it wasn't that.'

The other gave a shake of his head. 'I hadn't thought to tell anyone this,' he went on, 'but after what's happened to that poor girl…' he hesitated. 'Those difficulties you've been having - tricks going wrong, and such…'

He broke off as Sam stiffened. 'What about them?' He asked sharply.

'Well - they started here, didn't they? When that fellow came up on stage and pulled that toy snake out of his coat, caused a real to-do. Remember?'

'I'm unlikely to forget,' Sam told him. 'But what does that have to-'

'You didn't know,' the old stagehand broke in. 'So I'd best tell you. The bald cove – that loudmouth with the snake. He's Billy's uncle - name of Fred Bowes.'

'What? You mean, you know him?'

'I don't know him,' came the reply. 'Saw him once, in the pub with Billy. Bit of a villain, I thought…' he gave a shrug. 'You know what this business can be like. Someone's put stooges to mucking things up for you, haven't they? I've seen it before, Mr Vasey. You need to find out who it is, and stamp it out. Or who knows-'

'Where it'll end?' Sam finished bitterly. 'Supposing it ends with murder, Dan – will that be the last of it?'

The old man merely shook his head, laid a hand briefly on Sam's arm, and left him.

***

Late that afternoon, with a chilly autumn wind blowing, Sam returned home deflated. He had paid a few calls, asked around among people he knew, but instead of learning anything further he was more puzzled than ever. His work, along with his life it seemed, was in a kind of limbo. He alighted from the hansom, paid the cabman and was walking to the front gate when, to his alarm, a figure stepped out quickly from beneath a tree. The man was muffled in coat and scarf with his hat pulled low, and at first he did not know him.

'Mr Vasey… I beg pardon. I didn't mean to startle you.'

Sam blinked, and recognised Paulo Brunner.

'I didn't want to come inside, you see, with all the, er…' as always, the young man began to speak fast. 'To disturb your father at this time, I mean. I just… I had to catch you. I saw your man Durrell earlier, on his way out. He said you'd be back, didn't know when…'

Now Sam saw that he was shivering. 'How long have you been waiting?' He asked.

'An hour, perhaps…' Paulo swallowed nervously. 'As I said, I didn't want to bother you…' and when Sam gestured to the front door, he shook his head.

'No, I won't. I just wanted to… it's difficult, you see. I'm in a fix, and-'

'You mean, you need money?' Sam broke in angrily. 'Lord above, of all the times…'

'No!' Paulo shook his head. 'It isn't that at all. I came to tell you something – you've been good to me, and I thought you should know. After this I'll be gone – I'm leaving the country. My father's family will help me.'

'You mean, Switzerland?' Sam frowned at him. 'I thought you were working for Hobbs…'

'No - not anymore.' The words came out in a rush, and with another shiver. There was a moment as Paulo seemed to be plucking up courage, then: 'He was trying to ruin you – spoil your father's act, I mean. I didn't know to begin with - I swear I didn't. But now…'

'What?' His anger rising, Sam stared at him. 'Are you saying-'

'I was no part of it,' Paulo broke in. 'I swear on my own life. I wouldn't even have known about it, if that wasn't for Cuddy Carter.' And when Sam's frown deepened, he nodded quickly. 'Him and Hobbs, they're thick as thieves. And that's not a bad description, either… he wanted to ruin your father, Hobbs did. So that he'd come begging to join the agency. He paid a fellow to wreck that trick he does with the magic walnut. I don't know how…'

'But I do,' Sam broke in. 'It was simple enough…' on impulse he seized Paulo's arm, causing him to flinch.

'Come with me,' he said. 'If you don't want to talk to my father, we'll go out the back. There's a building where we can get out of the wind. Will you at least do that? You owe me something, don't you?'

Paulo shivered again, then gave a nod.

***

In the outhouse, Sam did not turn on the electric light Albert had installed; nobody was allowed to see The Great Albertini's props, and he would have been angry at Sam admitting anyone. Instead he found an oil lamp, lit it and set it down in a corner. Here the two of them sat in its limited glow, while the juggler's son span his sorry tale of deception.

And the worst part of it was, that Nancy had been involved from the very beginning.

'He had a hold over her, did Hobbs,' the young man said, rubbing his hands together to warm them. 'I don't know what, but he forced her to meet him… almost three weeks ago, I believe. He gave her a simple choice: do what he asked, and she'd be paid more money than she made in six months. Refuse him, and he'd spread gossip about her all over town – through the Halls, he meant. And he'd tell your father she was keeping secrets from him. She'd lose her place, he told her. She must have believed him, or she wouldn't have done it, would she?'

'Go on', Sam said. He was gazing into the lantern's glow, outwardly calm. At last, things were starting to make sense.

'Well, the first time it was just a warning – a shot across the bows, so to speak. He arranged for someone to volunteer for that mind-reading trick, and…'

But when Sam let out an oath, he trailed off.

So that was it: Nancy hadn't needed to see through the blindfold after all, because she already knew about the snake. And after that, the failure of the Heavy-and-Light chest had not been a warning, but a clear threat. But as for the last event – the true catastrophe… he looked up, to see Paulo looking anxiously at him.

'You mentioned Cuddy Carter,' he said. 'What's his part in

it?'

'To tell the truth, he probably isn't involved,' came the reply. 'But he knows plenty of unsavoury types – pimps, thieves, all sorts. I think Hobbs only took him on because of that – being able to get men to do his dirty work, I mean. He didn't need another comic - let alone one as miserable as Carter.'

'But surely…' Sam was dismayed now. 'Surely Hobbs wouldn't stoop to such villainy as happened last Friday, at the Star? And I don't mean wrecking the illusion – I'm talking about what followed afterwards-'

'Oh no… please, don't even think it!'

At once Paulo sprang to his feet. 'No - Hobbs wouldn't have done that,' he blurted. 'Sabotage, yes… send a stooge in, yes. Force Nancy to ruin the show – but not-'

'Murder?' Sam finished 'I wouldn't have thought so either – but from what you've told me, I might think him capable of anything.'

'But not that, I'd swear it.' Paulo shook his head vigorously. 'You must believe me. What happened to poor Nancy has shaken all of them – Hobbs too. He's closed up the office, talks of going away for a while, as Carter has already-'

'He what?' Sam snapped. 'Why would he do that, unless he's involved?'

'Because he's a slum-rat, and it's in his nature,' Paulo answered. 'He knows the police will come sniffing round – likely they'd seize him on principle, given his reputation. He did a spell in jail, once. Now he's high-tailed it to King's Cross, to take the first train north, he said. He isn't well-known up there…'

'So, how do you know this?' Sam interrupted. 'You, who once accused Carter of murdering your father? I don't understand.'

'Drink,' Paulo said, with a look of contempt. 'He's been drinking more than ever, since he started working for Hobbs. When the news came about Nancy, he ducked out like a shot, headed for the nearest public house. I caught up with him - never saw him scared like that. He told me to get out too – run for it, he said. But I pressed him, bought him drinks until he told me… not everything, maybe, but enough. Now he's gone - and good riddance.'

After that, Paulo sagged as if his energy had ebbed away. Sitting down again, he gave a deep sigh – but Sam's mind was whirling.

'So, you're telling me that Hobbs arranged the sabotage – ruining tricks, culminating with a real disaster at The Star, and…'

'But he's not a murderer,' Paulo insisted. 'And even Carter, damn the fellow, wouldn't do that to Nancy. I can't think why anybody would. She was liked by everyone – she was loved. You know that as well as I do.'

This time Sam made no reply. He was thinking of what Nancy had told him, of Paulo's unwelcome advances… now, he understood somewhat better how unpleasant that would have been for her. Yet she had broken no law: merely feared for her reputation, given the narrowness of popular opinion. Even his father, he thought ruefully, might have been disapproving… an image arose, of Miss Willens facing him defiantly with arms folded.

'Well, one thing's clear,' he said at last. 'Nancy wasn't exactly liked by everyone, was she? Someone was prepared to take her life, most savagely… as they took your father's, and Chen-Li's, and another poor fellow who happened to be nearby at the wrong time.'

'What - you think it's the same person?' Paulo looked appalled.

'You've read the papers, haven't you? A murderer abroad, like the Whitechapel killer…'

'I know,' Paulo broke in. 'But I don't have much confidence in the police. Nor in their finding their man - any more than they could three years back.'

'Well, then…' Sam drew a long breath, then eyed him sternly. 'You're quitting the country, you say. Leaving the whole business behind - your father's murder unsolved. Let the police and others worry about it… it's no longer your affair. On the Continent, no doubt you can start afresh. Wander round the salons and casinos… charm ladies of fashion, while spending whatever money you've salvaged from the Brunner estate. Am I near the mark?'

There was no answer. Avoiding his gaze, Paulo got to his feet. Watched by Sam, he buttoned up his coat, donned hat and scarf. He took a step towards the door, then hesitated.

'That loan I made to you?' Sam said, remaining seated. 'Don't let it trouble you. You can keep it, buy yourself a first-class passage on the boat.'

Without a word, the juggler's son pulled open the door and disappeared into the dusk. Sam heard his footsteps recede, and let out a long breath.

He had learned a great deal that day, after all – and from unexpected sources. But it didn't make him feel any better.

TWELVE

The following morning, after a somewhat tense conversation at Highgate, Sam and Albert travelled down to Scotland Yard in pouring rain, and asked to see Inspector Maskell.

It was time to lay everything out, they had decided; or rather Sam had decided, and after hearing all that he had learned, his father had agreed. Moreover, no longer would Sam hold back about their silent house-guest, Louise Chen. What had begun more than two weeks before, with the death of Carl Brunner, had turned into something far worse and far murkier. And what the juggler's son had told Sam had put a different light on things. Though how a vicious campaign by an unscrupulous rival to ruin The Great Albertini's act might be connected to the crime of murder, left him troubled and mystified.

'You should have told us all this, Mr Vasey – long before now.'

Inspector Maskell was displeased, and at his most officious. Having heard a full account from Sam, he paced the office while the others remained seated. Sergeant Drewe, at his desk, kept silent.

'In fact,' Maskell went on, 'most of what you've told me isn't new. We've not been idle, I assure you. And we've already seen Miss Poole's friend in Islington. Her testimony concurs with what you say.'

Sam glanced at his father, who sat with eyes lowered. After their talk that morning, he had left Sam to take charge.

'As for Lysander Hobbs…' the inspector wore a distasteful look. 'We spoke to him some time ago, as a man with strong connections in the Music Halls. He made a number of suggestions. Though none of them, I should say, have borne fruit.'

That was no surprise to Sam. He pictured the man in his comfortable office, pouring sherry. Beside him, he felt Albert tense: he would never forgive Hobbs for what he had done.

'But in the matter of Miss Poole's death…' Maskell paused.

'We have suspicions, but-'

'They're nothing more than that – and none of them hold water.'

Sergeant Drewe spoke abruptly, regarding his superior without expression. While the inspector bridled, he faced Sam.

'I see that you've tried to help, Mr Vasey, as you said you would. And we're grateful – are we not, sir?' He added, with a brief glance at Maskell. 'But the fact remains, in the absence of witnesses our hands are tied. Nobody appears to have a motive for any of these murders – apart from that of Harold Holcombe, who could have posed a threat to Chen-Li's killer. However…' He turned to the inspector. 'In view of what you've now told us, about your sheltering Mrs Chen-'

'I was coming to that, sergeant.'

Irritated by his subordinate's taking over the conversation, Maskell strode to Drewe's desk and leaned on it. 'That was most remiss of you, gentlemen,' he continued, eying Albert and Sam in turn. 'The widow is a vital witness – and from what I can see, you've been harbouring her as if she were a fugitive! Did it not occur to you that we needed to question her?'

'It crossed my mind, inspector,' Sam answered. 'But she came as a friend, shocked and bereaved… she was desperate. Should we have turned her away? Would you have turned her away, in such circumstances?'

'That's beside the point,' Maskell replied. 'Now that we know where she is – which could almost amount to kidnap in the eyes of the law, or at the least obstruction of our enquiries – we will interview her without further delay. Is that clear?'

'Inspector, if you please.'

All three men turned to Albert, who had yet to utter a word. Lifting his gaze, he eyed Maskell calmly enough. 'We understand your position,' he said. 'We meant no harm – quite the reverse. The woman was afraid – she is still. But of whom, she won't tell… even to my son, whom she seems to trust. Perhaps you may succeed where we haven't.'

A moment passed. Surprised by his conciliatory tone, Sam threw a look of approval at his father, then spoke up.

'If I might make a request, inspector?' And when Maskell

turned to him: 'Instead of summoning Mrs Chen here, would you consider seeing her at our home? I think she feels safe there – perhaps she'll speak now. Believe me, her presence has been difficult for us all.'

With that, he waited. And though he was relieved when, after some frowning, the inspector gave a nod, he nevertheless felt uneasy. Whatever emerged from this maelstrom, he thought briefly, might well be something none of them wanted to hear.

By the time they rose to take their leave, however, it was settled: Maskell and Drewe would come to Highgate that same afternoon. As for the business of sabotage, which indeed appeared to be a deliberate campaign by Lysander Hobbs: to the inspector it was of little importance. Did the Vaseys wish to bring charges? He enquired. If so, it would be difficult to specify what crimes had in fact been committed, let alone prove them…

Once again, it appeared, evidence was lacking.

***

For The Great Albertini and his company, that day would bring revelations that were more than unexpected: in the end, they were astonishing.

After a hasty luncheon, they gathered in the lounge: Albert, Sam and Louise Chen. The officers duly arrived, and sat down facing her. Bradby was in the house, to be within call if needed. The props man, who had taken Nancy's death very hard, had rarely spoken of late. But after hearing Alice's accounts of silent telephone calls, and of footsteps heard outside at night, he had busied himself fitting new locks to windows. For now, it seemed to be enough.

Once the inspector had taken his seat, he got swiftly to work - and it seemed he was in no humour to make allowances for Louise Chen's recent tragedy.

'I wish you'd spoken to us sooner, madam,' he began. 'Your reticence - your reluctance, I could say, might well have allowed a murderer to escape. Can you not see that?'

To his annoyance, the lady made no reply. Though she had discarded the veil she had worn during her early days in the house, she was still in mourning black, her eyes downcast.

'Come – this won't do,' Maskell persisted. 'I agreed to conduct our interview here out of consideration to you – but if you won't co-operate, I can have you taken into custody. Now, do you understand?'

'Yes… I understand.' She sighed, then looked up. 'But I am a French citizen, sir, and I have committed no crime. Perhaps you should speak to my embassy.'

'If necessary, we will,' was the inspector's reply. 'Though I hope it won't come to that.' With an effort, he added: 'I know you have suffered a great loss, in terrible circumstances. But your husband was not the only victim, hence-'

'I know that, of course,' Madame Chen said quickly. 'This family – my kind hosts, have also suffered.' Somewhat to Sam's surprise, she threw a kindly look towards him. It was the first real sign of gratitude, he realised, that she had ever expressed.

'Well then, don't you want to assist us in catching the perpetrator?' Maskell demanded.

'Catch him?' The lady sighed again. 'If only it were so simple.'

'What do you mean?' The inspector was losing patience. 'This sounds like evasion, madam. I demand that you tell me what you know, and stop wasting time.'

All eyes were on the woman, and for once Sam saw her wavering. What compelled her to such reluctance he could not know, but following Nancy's death the time for being taciturn was past. He would have spoken, had Sergeant Drewe not intervened.

'We're here to help you, madam,' he said. 'All of London wants to see this murderer caught – and you're probably the only person who saw him at close quarters. For all our sakes, will you not help us in return? It's a matter of-'

'Mon Dieu - do you not think I would do so, if I could?'

Startling everyone, the woman snapped out the words, cutting Drewe short. In the silence that fell, she looked quickly from the officers to Sam and to Albert. Putting a hand to her forehead, she closed her eyes briefly, then:

'They are not murderers,' she said, forcing herself to look at the inspector. 'Or, not in the way you think. They are simply carrying out orders – doing their appointed task. Only, they made a mistake, and are trying to put it right.'

Taken aback, the men regarded her in silence.

'As for seeing the one who shot my husband at close quarters, as you say… it was dark, and it was all over quickly. But yes, perhaps I could identify him. And if he had not been distracted, and shot that poor man who was standing near, I too would be dead! But then…' she lowered her gaze. 'In the end, it makes little difference. Even if he were caught, another would come in his place. Their task is to remove me, and only then will they cease.'

'Good God… this is intolerable!'

It was Albert who spoke – angrily, his voice filling the room. Thus far he had sat in silence; now, he gazed fiercely at Louise. 'Are you saying that this… this person, or persons, whoever they are, intend to come here to murder you too?' He demanded. 'Don't you see that this puts my entire household in danger?' He glanced at Sam. 'In fact, from what my son tells me, it appears there's been an intruder prowling about already – and yet you've said nothing? After we took you in, gave you shelter-'

'Father, please.'

At Sam's intervention the great conjuror broke off, breathing hard.

'Madame Chen…' Sam turned to the lady. 'You cannot stop now, after what you've said. Please, for our sake if no-one else's, tell these officers what you know, and let them do their work.'

'Otherwise,' Albert put in, with a dark look, 'I'll have no choice but to ask you to find accommodation elsewhere.'

But at that, Louise Chen nodded. 'So be it, sir,' she replied gravely. 'And you are right… I am humbled, after all you have done for me. I will make arrangements to leave at once.'

'Not just yet, if you please.'

Inspector Maskell got to his feet and took a pace forward, making her flinch.

'I will agree with what both Mr Vaseys have said,' he conceded. 'So, for everyone's sake, tell me what you know -

now. Or else…' as a thought struck him, he hesitated, then: 'Or, it may not be possible for you to attend your husband's funeral.' And when the lady drew a sharp breath, he added: 'His body is at the mortuary, and with the inquest over the burial may take place. But if, as you say, you are at risk from someone bent on your destruction-'

'How can you be so cruel, monsieur!'

At once, she too stood up. 'But then, you cannot understand…' the lady faltered - and quite suddenly, to the relief of both policemen and the Vaseys, she appeared to make a decision.

'Very well… I will give my testimony, and you may act upon it – if you can,' she told the inspector. 'But you will not prevent me from putting my husband to rest – I would die first.'

Whereupon, watched by them all, she resumed her seat and began.

***

The first surprise was that Chen-Li was not Chinese after all, but a Russian subject.

It was Bradby, Sam recalled, who had once raised a fleeting suspicion as to the late juggler's identity – *has anyone ever seen him without his pigtail and make-up*? Now, along with the others in the room, he listened in near amazement.

'And I am not Madame Chen,' the lady announced. 'My name is Sidorov – Louise Sidorov, and my husband was Danya.' She smiled sadly. 'The greatest juggler in Russia, some said – a star of the Circus. I speak of the Nikitin, most famous in his country.'

Sam glanced at his father: even in England, those in their circle had heard of the celebrated Nikitin Brothers' Circus.

'So that's why he never spoke,' Albert said, after a moment. 'Because he would have given himself away.'

She gave a little shrug. 'His English is poor, as his accent is strong. He was a fugitive already, when we met…' she seemed to be remembering as she spoke. 'In Paris that was, where he had travelled in haste, and where he took a new name and a new persona – and since he could do no other, he worked as a juggler. When that name was discovered, we came to London and he took another – Chen-Li. Performing was his life, sirs, and you know how skilled he was. The best – I've heard many in London say it.'

'One moment, please.' Maskell was gazing at her with suspicion. 'You say he was a fugitive from Russia - do you mean from the law?'

Madame Sidorov – for such, they had now learned, was her name – met his eye coolly.

'The law?' She echoed, with a bitter little laugh. 'In Russia, monsieur, the Tsar is the law… I speak of the tyrant Alexander. Woe to any man who dares talk against him – even in jest, or in drink. And for a brave man like Danya, who did more than just talk - who dared to consort with others who try to resist the Tsar's brutal rule, more than mere woe may follow. I speak of arrest, imprisonment in the harshest of conditions, then almost certain execution-'

'That's quite enough, madam!' Angrily, the inspector raised his hand. 'I'm not here to listen to political speeches. What happened in Russia or in Paris is not my concern. We're investigating a series of murders - in London.'

'And I say to you, monsieur,' Louise Sidorov retorted, 'that these men were not bent on murder, but on execution carried out under orders. And since you have still not divined the truth, I will tell you. The assassins' target, of course, was my husband – but it's likely they knew only that he was a juggler, working in London under an assumed name. And so…'

'They killed Carl Brunner – by mistake.'

It was Sam who spoke, as in that moment the truth struck him. Of course, no-one had a real motive to kill Brunner: even his son, whatever their relations may have been. Despite what Cuddy Carter had told him, he never believed Paulo capable of such – nor Carter, for all his sins. Now at last, it made sense.

And Louise merely nodded, lowering her eyes.

'But this is dreadful!' Maskell was staring at her. 'You mean, Brunner's murder was a case of mistaken identity? Is that what you implied, when you said they had to put it right? For if so they've surely succeeded, have they not? Once your husband was killed…'

'Their task is yet unfinished,' the lady broke in, without looking up. 'I saw the man who did it – but even had I not, their intention would have been to remove me. In Paris…' she faltered, as if frowning at some memory. 'Let us say that I am in possession of too much knowledge - for the man I loved, I would have braved anything. I shared his secrets, his passion for justice – I do so still. I'm certain the order would have been to kill us both. As I told you, I am lucky to be alive.'

'The order?' Maskell echoed. 'You keep repeating that, yet I'm in the dark still. For pity's sake, madam, tell me – *whose* orders are they? And who are these men?'

Everyone was looking at her. She hesitated, then lifted her head.

'They are the *Okhrana*,' she replied. 'The Tsar's secret police, who serve him without question. They almost caught us in Paris…' she drew a breath, then: 'I can well imagine the fury of their master – Rachkovsky, of the Okhrana's French office. His instructions to his men would have been clear: to follow us to London and kill us both, and not to return until it was done. And there is no use asking me where they might be hiding, for I have no idea.'

'And so, your life is indeed in mortal danger - Mrs Sidorov.'

Louise turned sharply to Albert, who was eying her with a new respect.

'Now I understand better,' he said quietly. 'And I see that your fears are justified. I apologise for my harsh words – and the offer of a haven here remains. If you'd confided in us sooner, perhaps…' he drew a breath. 'But leaving that aside, we must confer – all of us - and see what may be done to protect you.' He looked pointedly at Sergeant Drewe, then at Maskell. 'Would you not agree, gentlemen?'

The inspector merely looked away; for once, he appeared helpless.

***

Plans were suggested, that same afternoon at the Vaseys' house - but they were at best optimistic, at worst foolish. That was Inspector Maskell's opinion, and he refused to sanction any of them. His intention was to go immediately to the

Commissioner of Police, Sir Edward Bradford, who would talk to others and eventually, he expected, to the Russian Embassy in Belgrave Square. This was now a diplomatic matter, he stated – perhaps graver even than the death of Carl Brunner, which had now been overshadowed. Moreover, he warned both Sam and Albert not to involve themselves further in the business. But since he had no other immediate solution, he would agree to Louise Sidorov remaining at their home for the present. His suggestion of stationing an officer there, however, was firmly rejected by The Great Albertini.

'This house is quite secure,' Albert had told him. 'My man Bradby Durrell is utterly reliable as a bodyguard, and will remain here for the foreseeable future. Should any intruder be discovered, we will of course summon the police at once.'

And so for the moment it was settled, the officers departing before dusk. The other thing they had agreed upon, despite Maskell's reservations, was that the funeral of Danya Sidorov would take place here in London: his widow insisted upon it, refusing all suggestions of his body being sent elsewhere – even to his home country. In the matter of a police presence at the burial, however, she had no choice: Maskell would station men at the church and at the graveside under cover, given the possibility that the men of the Tsar's secret police would learn of the funeral, and try to carry out their orders.

'Yet I dislike it wholeheartedly, Mr Vasey - and if I could, I would prevent it,' were his final words to Sam, before taking his leave. 'We are in effect using Mrs Sidorov as bait – which goes against everything I believe in.'

Once he and the sergeant had gone, Sam and his father took to the parlour where whiskeys were soon poured, and Bradby was called in. Louise, after expressing her thanks to them both, had once again retired to her room. Though now that all was out in the open, Sam noticed a lessening of tension in their guest, that was almost akin to relief.

'I'll make the funeral arrangements,' he said. 'Louise will repay us, she says. She'll sell her house eventually, and leave England… she's not sure where she'll go.'

'You mean, provided she lives to do so,' Albert said. Since

the lady's revelations he had brooded on the matter, as if almost regretting his decision to help her further.

'I'll be right beside her,' Bradby said at once. 'And if anyone tries to-'

'No!' Albert eyed him, shaking his head. 'I won't have you blundering in. We'll protect her, of course. But if these… these men dare to appear, you must let the police act.'

Bradby drew a deep breath; he was struggling, and Sam saw it.

'I know what you're thinking,' he said gently. 'All the talk has been about Chen-Li's murder… or Sidorov's, I should say. It's as if what happened to Nancy is of less importance.'

'Not to me, it isn't,' Bradby replied.

'Nor to me,' Albert said sharply. 'I won't be able to rest until the culprit's found, and yet…' frowning, he turned to Sam. 'I'm as confused as I ever was. Surely even these Russian devils wouldn't have done that? I mean, what possible reason could they have?'

Sam had no answer. In fact, Nancy's murder had been touched upon earlier by Sergeant Drewe, before the officers had left. Though it was of small surprise to him that they were no closer to identifying a culprit, let alone a reason for the savage act.

'We won't let it rest,' he said at last. 'With what we know now – her being forced to work for Hobbs, and the rest of it – there's still a lot needs explaining. She was scared towards the end, her friend told me, and I'm not sure why.'

'I don't want you playing detective again,' Albert said firmly 'Once this… this business is over – I mean the funeral, after which I hope Mrs Sidorov will be able to leave – we must get back to work. What else is there?'

As if for support he turned to Bradby, but the other would not meet his eye. Instead he lifted his glass, drained it and stood up rather briskly.

'I've got things to do,' he said. ''You'll be wanting the carriage, I suppose – when everything's arranged, I mean?'

He meant the funeral. Sam nodded, and threw him a kindly look. After their man had left the room, he faced Albert.

'It won't be easy, starting again,' he said. 'Though I know you can do it – *we* can do it,' he added. 'But I've never seen Bradby brought as low as this. I wasn't even sure he'd want to stay, but it seems he does. We're family to him – the only one he has.'

'In which case, we're now a bereaved family,' Albert said.

'And so…' Sam sat upright, with a determined look. 'I say again, an American tour might be the best solution – and no, it's not cowardly,' he added swiftly, seeing the look that appeared. 'It would merely give us a clean break. And we wouldn't even have to find a new Mirabel immediately… we could hire one in America. Will you at least consider it?'

Albert met his eye, with Sam expecting an angry riposte. Instead, his father gave a nod.

And soon after that they parted, Sam going at once to the office. But it was not The Great Albertini's business that would preoccupy him, not yet. There was a funeral to arrange, for a deceased Russian whom the Music Hall world had known as Chen-Li, the taciturn but brilliant Chinese juggler.

As he sat down at his desk, he saw again the face of the man's grieving widow. He had offered to do this, he thought, and he would make every effort not to disappoint her.

THIRTEEN

The morning of the funeral - the following Monday - dawned bright, sunlit and calm; a perfect autumn day. Sam was thankful for that, at least. It was in his thoughts as the party assembled in the leaf-strewn cemetery in Islington, after a brief service in the church. It was the place where Nancy had been laid to rest: a poignant reminder for the Vaseys. They, Bradby and the deceased's widow were the only mourners – apart from Edgar Downs, manager of the Tivoli Palace of Varieties. In his black coat and top hat with mourning band, the man stood at Sam's side while the parson did his office.

'I'm here on behalf of all my staff,' he said, speaking low. 'There were others who wanted to come and pay their respects, but in view of everything I put them off. Chen-Li may not have been liked by all, but he was admired – perhaps more than he realised.'

Sam nodded; as far as Downs and almost everyone else knew, the late juggler was still Chen-Li and would remain so.

'I gather no arrests have been made,' the Tivoli's manager went on. 'A direful business – and still an utter mystery to us all.'

Uneasily, Sam looked away; he had promised Inspector Maskell to say nothing to anyone of what Louise Sidorov had revealed. His glance fell on the widow, veiled and swathed in black, standing beside the open grave with head bowed. Albert and Bradby stood close, one on either side of her. Bradby's eyes roved about restlessly, as if daring anyone to approach. Further off, two policemen in plain clothes were on similar watch, under the orders of Sergeant Drewe who was outside the cemetery, at the roadside. There was only one entrance, and no stranger could appear without drawing attention.

Sam had taken a moment to speak to Drewe, and learned only one thing of note: that the Russian Embassy claimed to know nothing of the Tsar's secret police, and denied all knowledge of any covert operations. Inspector Maskell, unsurprisingly, was furious.

There came a stirring among the little group, as the parson finished his service and closed his book. When he turned to Louise Sidorov, she nodded but began to walk towards the gates; it seemed she had no wish to wait for the coffin to be covered. The Vaseys' carriage was waiting, a hired coachman in black at the reins. After saying a few words to Edgar Downs, Sam followed his father and Bradby, who were keeping close to their charge. But there seemed no cause for concern; the only bystanders near the gates were those who had stopped out of respect, the men with hats removed. As the party emerged on to the pavement, people stood back; passing carriages slowed down, drivers touching their caps.

From nowhere, Sergeant Drewe appeared at Sam's side.

'I thought it would prove a false alarm,' he murmured. 'If these damned assassins are skilled at their work, they'd know better than to show up here in broad daylight. Their sort strike by night – quick and efficient.'

Privately, Sam had thought the same. But since Maskell was taking no chances, he had gone along with it all. The priority now was to get Louise back to Highgate safely. He watched as she, Bradby and Albert got into the carriage, then went to the door. He was about to close it, when Albert spoke from inside.

'We'll see her home,' he said. 'Why don't you take a breather, then come back to the house? Alice has prepared a funeral breakfast.'

'A breather?' Sam frowned – then caught Bradby's eye. The prop man was trying to signal past Sam's shoulder. Glancing round, he saw Edgar Downs approaching Sergeant Drewe, clearly about to engage him in conversation.

'Well… if you're sure,' he said. He turned to Louise Sidorov, sitting opposite her guardians and seemingly composed. Lifting her veil, the lady met his eye.

'You have my heartfelt thanks, monsieur,' she said quietly. 'After all that you've done, I will be forever grateful. And I know Danya would wish me to express the same sentiment.'

Whereupon a look passed between them that startled him: was it more than one of mere gratitude? With a polite nod, he turned to face Albert.

'You go on ahead, then,' he said. 'Perhaps I could do with a walk after all, stretch my legs.'

Stepping back, he closed the carriage door and signalled to the coachman to drive on.

A few minutes later, having interrupted Downs and Drewe who were merely exchanging a few words, he found himself being invited for a drink. The one who invited him, however, was neither of those men. Having bidden them farewell, seen Downs hail a cab and Drewe walk off with his constables, he was moving away when a hand landed on his sleeve. Turning sharply, he found himself facing John Chambers, the stage manager of the Tivoli.

'I didn't mean to disturb you,' Chambers said. 'I wouldn't come in the church. Downs didn't want me here anyway… things are still a bit tense at the Tiv, with all that's happened.' And when Sam regarded him, he added: 'I heard you came round last week. I've been talking with some of the boys, like old Dan Swift. He said he'd spoken to you, so I thought maybe you and I should have a quiet word.'

'I see.' Sam paused. 'Well, as it happens I'm free at present.'

'Good,' the other said briskly. 'What about the Angel? Not far, is it?'

***

The Angel was an old coaching inn on the corner of Islington High Street and Pentonville Road. When Sam and John Chambers entered, the place was already growing lively with mid-day customers and dense with tobacco smoke. Chambers bought glasses of beer, and after they had found a corner to themselves, he came quickly to the point.

'It's young Billy Bowes,' he said quietly. 'I thought there was something odd going on, those few days before Brunner was killed. The lad had more money to spend than usual, for one thing - moreover, his mind wasn't always on his job. Now I hear rumours about Lysander Hobbs playing dirty tricks on your father…' and when Sam's eyes narrowed, he added: 'Word gets round, you know. I've been in the Music Hall business a long time - I believe I know who to trust and who to be wary of. In short, I'm no longer sure of Billy – and his taking off as he has done, clinches it for me.'

'You mean, you think Hobbs was using him?'

'I can't be sure, but Billy comes from a rough family. Jailbirds, some of them.'

'Good God.' Sam let out a breath. 'The uncle, who-'

'Nearly ruined your father's mind-reading act,' Chambers finished. 'Dan told me… I wish I'd known. It would have been easy enough to hire a man like Fred Bowes to do what he did.'

'But from what I've gathered, that piece of sabotage was only a warning,' Sam said, thinking fast. 'Even if the Bowes were involved, far worse happened at the Daisy-Cup and The Star.'

'So I heard,' came the reply. 'And if you want my advice, you should try asking a few questions at The Star.' With that, he glanced away and took a drink.

'Why? Is there something I should know?'

Chambers paused, then: 'Let's say Lysander Hobbs has a long arm these days, shall we? I make no accusations, of course…' he lowered his gaze. 'But between ourselves, I wouldn't trust Jack Coates either.'

'You wouldn't?' Sam eyed him keenly.

'Not an inch,' came the reply.

'But this just throws up more questions,' Sam said, mulling it over. 'A campaign to bring my father down is bad enough, even if we could prove it. Nancy's murder, however, is beyond all reason…'

'As was the killing of two jugglers,' Chambers murmured.

For a moment, Sam was almost tempted to tell the man what he knew about those particular events, but overcame the notion. He took a drink, then returned to the topic of Billy Bowes.

'You and I saw Bowes, after he found Brunner's body,' he said. 'He was shaken to the core – and that was no play-acting. Now you say he was even more jittery, after-'

'After Nancy was killed, especially,' Chambers broke in. 'Then, Billy might be a bit of a villain, but he's no murderer.'

'Yet, he disappeared at once, and hasn't been seen since.'

'Scared,' Chambers said. 'Maybe he thought Hobbs had gone way too far. Or one of his men got carried away, or…' he gave a shrug. 'I don't envy you, with your troubles,' he added. 'If I could help you, I would. But I'm a cautious man, Sam Vasey. And I've learned that there are times, in this business, when you simply have to look the other way.'

'I was told Hobbs had tried to persuade Brunner to join his agency, without success,' Sam said. 'However, I…' he framed his words carefully. 'I'm certain he wouldn't stoop to murder. Too much to lose.'

Chambers gave a nod. 'True… and I think I've told you all I can. Just thought I'd pass on a few thoughts.'

'I thank you, John,' Sam said.

'For what?' The other raised his eyebrows. 'We're just a couple of Music Hall men having a drink, aren't we? Now, if it's all the same to you, I'd better be on my way.'

And a short while later, outside the Angel, they parted with a handshake. Downs headed down City Road to catch an omnibus, while Sam turned left into Islington High Street.

He crossed the junction with Liverpool Road, barely noticing that people were hurrying by with umbrellas. It had started to rain; absently, he pulled his collar up and quickened his pace. The Star… perhaps he should have returned there already, he thought, no matter how unwelcome he might be; the matter of the electro-magnet being disconnected had never truly been addressed. And after what John Chambers had said about Coates… mulling the matter over, he heard a cab draw up beside the pavement, and a voice call out.

'Mr Vasey - over here!'

He turned to see a hansom lurching to a halt, the door slightly open.

'Get in!' Someone shouted. 'Or do you want to get soaked?'

He stepped towards the vehicle, glancing up at the cabman on his seat at the rear. The man was staring straight ahead, muffled in his cape. Peering in, Sam made out a hatted figure.

'Do I know you, sir?' He asked - then froze.

From inside the cab, a revolver was pointed directly at his face.

'I said get in,' the occupant murmured. 'Slow and casual, eh?

***

They drove for perhaps fifteen minutes, turning into Essex Road and then proceeding to Balls Pond Road, heading towards Dalston. All the while they sat in silence: Sam upright and rigid, the other beside him holding the revolver. He had a scarf pulled up, concealing most of his face. Traffic flew past in the wet streets, the cabman whipping his horse to a brisk canter. There was no use in trying to address his captor, Sam thought; doubtless he would soon learn why this was happening. He was breathing steadily: in a way, he decided, he almost relished a confrontation - at least he might get some answers. Steeling himself, he was thrown forward when the cab suddenly lurched to a halt.

'Out you get,' said the man, opening the door with his free hand. Sam clambered out, finding himself in a cobbled yard between semi-derelict buildings. In fact, he was not far from where he had grown up, yet the place was unfamiliar. Looking about, he saw nailed-up doors and broken windows, whereupon a shove sent him staggering forward.

'Straight ahead,' came the order, and at that moment a door creaked open on the other side of the yard. A slim figure appeared in a cap and coat, a scarf tied across his face too. Sam was marched to the entrance, finding himself entering an empty stable. Behind him he heard the cabman crack his whip, and with a clatter of hooves the hansom drove away.

He glanced round while his eyes adjusted to the gloom. There was a Jacob's ladder in the corner leading to a hay-loft, and a loose-box to one side. Otherwise there was just assorted clutter and old straw, dank and mouldy. He barely had time to observe his surroundings before he was thrust forward on to his knees, sending his hat flying.

'Sit down there,' came the order from his captor. 'Against the wall.'

Turning about, breathing hard, Sam sat on the floor with his back to a rough wall. The two men had found barrels, and both sat down facing him. The one with the revolver rested it on his knee, keeping a firm grip in his fist.

'No need to cack your britches,' the slight fellow in the coat said, in a tone of cocky amusement. 'We just wanted a word, is all.'

Sam kept silent, and waited.

'You've been a busy man, Vasey,' the other one said. 'Far too busy, in fact. I'd have thought someone in your position would be a sight more careful.'

'I've no idea what you mean,' Sam said. They were the first words he had spoken since being forced into the cab. His mouth was dry, and the stable was dusty. He forced himself to salivate, managing not to cough, and tried to gather his wits.

'The juggler's wife – I should say, the late juggler,' the man went on. 'The Frenchwoman, I'm talking about.' He spoke as the senior; the other - a younger man – seemed to be an accomplice.

'Who?' Sam asked innocently. Having accepted his predicament, he was beginning to feel a powerful resentment towards these two, whoever they were. His query, however, produced an immediate retort

'Don't try any of that!' The older man snapped, lifting his revolver. 'We've brought you here to deliver fair warning – and you're lucky it's nothing more. So listen!'

'I think he could do with a bit of persuasion,' the younger one said, keeping his eyes on Sam. 'He don't seem to realise it's serious.'

Suddenly, Sam stiffened: he knew that voice. He didn't recall where he had heard it before, but...

'He knows it's serious,' the older one said, with a trace of irritation.

Sam looked keenly from one to the other: there was tension between them. Moreover, he believed he was in more danger from the unarmed one than from his superior. He saw the cold glitter in the young man's eyes, and guessed that he was keen enough to deal out what he called *persuasion*.

'Your instructions, which I'm bound to deliver, are these,' said his older captor. 'You and your father are being a nuisance, Vasey, mixing yourself up in that woman's affairs. So, it's plain enough: put her out of your house and forget about her. She's nothing but trouble.'

'She's been no trouble to us,' Sam said quietly.

'Now you listen to me,' came the sharp reply. 'This isn't a conversation, it's a friendly warning. Do as you're told, and our business is finished. Make difficulties, and you're in more of a pickle than you can handle. So, how do you want it – sensible, or stupid?'

'Is it you who's been making phone calls, then ringing off?' Sam asked, on impulse. 'Or wandering around the house at night? Worried our housekeeper, that did. You wouldn't want to get on the wrong side of her.'

'Well, well… it looks to me like he wants to be stupid.'

The younger man stood up quickly, his shoulders tense. He took a step towards Sam, prompting his fellow to turn angrily.

'Shut your mouth and sit down,' he ordered.

'I say we give him a slap or two, make him see sense,' the other argued.

'Why don't you try it?' Sam said at once. It was reckless, but he saw a glimmer of opportunity. Scrambling to his feet, he went into a boxer's crouch.

The response was a burst of raucous laughter.

'Will you look at him?' The young man jeered, jerking his thumb towards Sam. 'He thinks it's a game! Come on then, mister – let's see you make a fool of yourself!'

And before his companion could react, he raised a fist and came forward – whereupon for Sam, the penny dropped at last.

'My God, I know you,' he breathed. 'You're Arthur – you played the ape, and ran off!'

It was true; and for a moment, there was a silence in which nobody moved. For Sam, it all came back with a rush: the cheeky young man in the dressing-room at The Star, roaring and beating his chest; Albert looking disapproving – and the look that passed between Arthur and Nancy. Then the catastrophe that followed, when both she and the ape had disappeared…

'Oh, fuck this.'

The older man got abruptly to his feet, with an air more of resignation than of anger. Startled, his junior turned - to be dealt a blow across the face with the barrel of the revolver. He staggered, fell backwards and sat down on his rump in the straw.

'For once, will you just do as you're told and nothing more?'

His assailant cried, waving the gun at him. 'Or would you rather have a slap or two yourself?'

For a moment, his attention was not on Sam; it was a half-chance at best, but it was all he would get. Without allowing himself to think, he lunged at his captor and cracked him on the jaw. When the man reeled, he seized his arm and wrenched it backwards with all his strength.

There was a sickening crack as the bone broke, and a yell of pain, whereupon Sam seized his advantage. He barely saw the gun fall to the floor, as he leaped to the nearest barrel and lifted it. Fortunately, it was empty – and a second later, he had brought it crashing down on his victim's head. Without a sound, the man crumpled and fell like a limp sack.

But it wasn't over, of course.

Whirling round, Sam side-stepped instinctively to see Arthur, on hands and knees, making a grab for the revolver where it lay. Sam stamped on his hand, producing a cry of mingled pain and rage, while stooping for the weapon. But he failed: Arthur seized his leg and yanked it aside, making him lose balance. As he fell, he caught the other's wrist – and in a moment they were both in the straw, wrestling for possession of the gun.

Mercifully, the tussle was brief. Arthur was strong and wiry, but Sam was desperate. Grabbing his opponent's hand, he bent it back, each of them struggling to grasp the weapon. Finally, Sam delivered a kick to Arthur's side, which bought him a split second's advantage. Letting go of his wrist, he punched him hard on the cheek, making him yelp. And when the man's grip loosened, he snatched the gun from him and tore himself free.

Panting, covered in bits of straw, Sam got clumsily to his knees and raised the gun. His face screwed up in pain, Arthur got to his knees too. His scarf had come off during the struggle. Breathlessly, the two of them eyed each other - whereupon a savage grin appeared on the young man's face.

'You won't use that,' he grunted, gesturing to the revolver. 'You couldn't.'

Slowly he stood up, glancing at his companion who was sprawled nearby, clearly unconscious. 'Sweet Jesus, but you're a lucky one, chum,' he added. 'And you've got no idea just how lucky.'

Still pointing the gun, Sam too stood up. 'Who are you working for, Arthur?' He asked, trying to sound calm. 'Lysander Hobbs, or someone else?'

His answer was a mere shake of the head.

'Till next time, Sammy boy,' Arthur said.

And with a look of scorn, he started for the door. Taking a breath, Sam held the revolver out, aiming it at his chest - but it was no use. He could never shoot a man in cold blood, and the other knew it. He was one who had done bad things, and would doubtless do more. *A slum-rat…* Paulo Brunner's expression flew to his mind. Where Nancy had found this hard-nosed youth, he was unsure – unless it was through Hobbs. He watched as, with a look of contempt, Arthur raised his hand with fingers pointed at Sam's head, and with his mouth made the sound of a gunshot. Then he turned and hurried out of the stable. Sam heard his footsteps splashing on wet cobbles, breaking from a walk into a run, until he was gone.

For a moment he stood still, his mind whirling. He could barely grasp the fact that he had been taken at gunpoint, brought here to be scared away from helping Louise Sidorov, and had managed to overcome both his captors. *You're a lucky one, old chum…* Arthur's words rang in his head. He had indeed been lucky - but what should he do now? Still catching his breath, he turned to look down at Arthur's companion, who in the end had been somewhat careless in dealing with his impetuous henchman. His question as to who they worked for had gone unanswered - but in view of all that had happened of late, he had a strong suspicion.

These two, he guessed, were merely hired men: ruffians who cared little what they were asked to do, provided the payment was sufficient. The ones who had hired them, if Sam's suspicions were correct, were still at large – and so, Madame Sidorov was still in as much danger as before.

She would be back at Highgate, he thought, sitting down to a funeral breakfast. Whereas he was standing over the man who had ordered him to send her away, or face some serious but unnamed consequences.

It was troubling, but for Sam it was not a dilemma; it struck him then that he had known it for days, perhaps longer. He could no more let Louise be harmed than he could his own father. He might even, he realised, be a little in love with her.

Hearing a sound from near his feet, he turned sharply - to see his former captor stir, then groan and put a shaky hand to his head.

FOURTEEN

Following the violent events of the past minutes, the situation was suddenly reversed. Seated on the barrel he had used to floor his captor, Sam regarded him as he struggled to a sitting position, wincing with pain. He had bent down to pull the scarf away, revealing a thin-faced, grey-moustached man, older than he had expected.

'You bastard,' the injured one muttered. 'You'll get your desserts, Vasey…'

'You'd better think of yourself,' Sam told him. 'You need someone to treat your arm. But first, I'd like to know who paid you to bring me here.'

'You can go to hell,' came the reply.

'Let me guess, then,' Sam went on. 'Might it be a foreigner – say, a Russian person?'

The other gave no answer, merely eyed him balefully.

'The matter is,' Sam said, feeling his anger rise, 'Just over a week ago, I lost someone who was close to me – murdered, her body left in an alley. Do you know anything about that?'

Once again there was no reply. But an uneasy expression passed quickly across the other's face, to be replaced by a scowl.

'We're talking about death by hanging, for such a crime,' Sam said. 'Even an accomplice might get the same – or a long sentence of hard labour, at least. So, to borrow your phrase: how do you want it - sensible, or stupid?'

'Damn you, Vasey!' The other spat, in sudden rage. 'You don't have a notion who you're dealing with – you're a dead man, after this.'

'So, you're choosing the stupid option?'

'I don't do murder!' the other threw back. 'And I don't know any Russians. Why don't you get out, and let me be?'

'I think not,' Sam replied. For a moment, he realised, he had almost forgotten he was holding the revolver. Now he raised it and pointed – only to receive a sneer in response.

'You haven't the grit,' his former captor said. 'You're a milksop – a girlie-boy from the Halls. Why don't you run home to your dad?'

For a moment Sam was torn. He wanted information from this ageing rogue, but he was also eager to forsake his company: to be back with Albert, and with Louise... then an idea occurred. 'I'll go out into the yard and fire the gun,' he announced, standing up. 'It shouldn't be long before I hear a policeman's whistle. If I don't, I'll fire it again and keep firing. That ought to bring someone running, don't you think?'

But for answer, the other gave a bark of laughter. 'Try it,' he said – at which realisation dawned on Sam: the weapon was not loaded. He wondered briefly if Arthur had known that – then realised that he had not.

'Go on, pull the bloody trigger!' The other growled, wincing again.

Breathing hard, Sam stepped to the doorway, pointed the revolver into the air and pulled the trigger, which produced nothing more than a heavy click.

'I told you I'm no murderer!' The old villain cried; clearly, the pain in his arm was worsening. Sam turned to see him trying to stand up, breathing in rasps. The opportunity was receding… thinking fast, he took a step outside and shouted at the top of his voice.

'Murder!' he yelled. 'Police! Murder!'

There was no answer, however; just a distant sound of horse traffic. Sam came back inside the stable, and decided to bluff. First, he moved quickly to his victim and shoved him back onto the floor, where he landed on his side with a cry of agony. Bending over him, Sam took hold of his good arm.

'Tell me something, and I might just let go,' he snapped, holding up the revolver. 'Otherwise, I'll take your other arm and make you squeal. Then I'll use this as a club, as you did to Arthur. When you're out cold again, I'll fetch the police. It's your choice – so decide.'

His answer was a hiss of pain. It struck him that the man was in poor shape… a petty criminal from the slums, far weaker than he had imagined.

'Speak up.' He ordered. 'You know you've lost, so tell me who sent you to warn me off.'

'Jesus' mercy…' wheezing, the other met his eye. 'Let me go, for pity's sake,' he muttered. 'I'm no use to you-'

'I'll decide that,' Sam broke in. 'I think you're working for the men who killed the Chinese juggler - and who intend to kill his widow. What's more, I think they might have killed Nancy Poole, though I'm not sure why-'

'They wouldn't, damn you! They'd no reason!'

The words flew out in a gasp, along with a stifled oath. Feebly, the other dropped his gaze.Sam looked down at him, his anger ebbing away.

'Then who did?' He demanded. 'If you know, you must tell me, or-'

He stopped himself, as both of them heard it: a police whistle, from not far away. It was followed by an answering whistle, further off: his shouts had been heard after all. Straightening himself, he regarded the oldster, whose criminal days were done.

'If you tell me what you know, I'll stall them,' he said. 'I might even say you were the accomplice, and the one who ran off was in charge. I could lose the gun too – you see?'

He gestured to a little heap of straw, where the revolver could be hidden. A moment passed, as the other peered up at him. He was wavering - then:

'You can go to blazes!' He growled, turning away. 'You bloody fool – do you think those men will let you live, after this? You and your blasted father? You were warned, but you wouldn't learn – now you're finished!'

And with a sigh he fell back on the dusty floor, putting a hand to his head. Gazing down at him, Sam heard footsteps outside, hurrying across the cobbles.

Someone called out, and at last he turned away.

***

Sergeant Drewe arrived at the Vasey house in mid-afternoon, after telephone calls had been made. Alice brought him to the drawing-room, where both Sam and Albert rose to receive him. Sam had bathed and changed his clothes since returning home by hansom; and though sobered by his experience, he was calm enough.

Albert, however, was angry, and in no mood to hold back.

'So much for police protection, sergeant,' he said, without preamble. 'My son could have been killed, or at least badly hurt. Moreover, it looks to me as if he's done the police's job, overpowering those murderous swine - and despite it all, the real perpetrators are still at large! Am I correct, or not?'

Drewe met his eye, then looked deliberately at Sam. 'How are you, Mr Vasey?' He enquired gently. 'Sounds like you've had quite a tussle.'

'I'm well enough,' Sam replied. 'Though I came away without learning much.'

The sergeant sighed and gave a nod. Sam gestured him to a chair, and they both sat. After a moment, Albert sat down too.

'You acted bravely, sir,' Drewe said, gazing frankly at Sam. 'The man we've apprehended is a known criminal – if somewhat long-in-the-tooth for such antics, I might say. His name's Alfred Gower, and he'll soon be back in prison. As for the other man, the one you knew as Arthur…' he shook his head. 'Gone, we don't know where. And Gower won't talk… call it criminals' code, if you like. That, or he's scared of what might happen if he turns Queen's Evidence.'

'Will Arthur be that difficult to find?' Sam asked, with a frown. Even as he spoke, he remembered that the one person who might have been able to tell him was dead. He glanced at his father, who sighed irritably.

'What an absolute farce this is,' Albert breathed. 'I resent being taken for a fool by these… these damned servants of the Tsar, or whoever they are. Who are they, to tell us to throw Madame Sidorov out? Meanwhile she's still in danger - as are we. It's intolerable.'

'I did offer to have a constable stationed here, for your protection,' the sergeant said mildly. 'The offer still stands – in fact, I'd recommend it.'

'It's something we should consider,' Sam said, eying his father. 'While our guest makes her arrangements, I mean.' Louise Sidorov, who had returned from the funeral sad and wearied, was resting in her room. But already she had spoken of leaving.

'Yes, yes…' Albert looked at Drewe. 'Let me sleep on it. I'd like to take time to assess our position - with my son, I mean. And my man Durrell will be here.'

'Very well, sir.' The sergeant stood up, facing Sam. 'Inspector Maskell will want to speak with you, after what happened. You may need to give evidence… as far as we know, there were no witnesses to your abduction. All anyone would have seen, is you getting into a cab.'

And that was how matters stood, for the present. After seeing Drewe out, Sam returned to the room to find Albert on his feet, pacing restlessly.

'We need to get ourselves out of this mire, Sam,' he said at once. 'We're not working – I'll be all but forgotten, if I don't get back on a stage soon. And you're merely getting yourself deeper into trouble, it appears. Those people seem to know our movements from one day to the next… the very thought makes me ill!'

Without answering, Sam sat down heavily. He had had many thoughts since his capture, but none seemed to offer any comfort. He saw again the drawn face of the ageing villain… and he saw Arthur, pointing an imaginary pistol and making the sound of a gunshot. Unbidden, his conversation with John Chambers sprang to mind… and a notion occurred.

'I told you what Chambers told me, about the people at The Star,' he said. 'That's where things came to a climax, was it not? The final straw, as regards sabotaging the act… Nancy disappearing, along with her so-called friend-'

'Don't mention that young devil's name to me,' Albert broke in harshly. 'If I had my way, he'd be boiled in oil!'

'I was thinking more about Jack Coates,' Sam told him. 'Chambers wouldn't trust him an inch, he said. I think we should go down to Bermondsey and ask questions. In fact…' he took a breath. 'I'm certain of it.'

'We?' Albert looked aghast. 'No, Sam – I'll not set foot in that Hall again. After that catastrophe, I just can't…' he trailed off, shaking his head.

But Sam had formed a resolve, and the decision gave him strength. 'I didn't mean you and I should go,' he said. 'I'm taking Bradby.'

***

By seven o'clock that evening The Star's performances were already under way. Sam and Bradby, having travelled down in a hansom, arrived at the Hall and entered by the stage door. The doorman recognised them but gave no greeting, merely frowned as they passed to the backstage area where there was the usual bustle. The orchestra were on fine form, accompanying a pair of female singers; a gaudy sign by the wings proclaimed *The Simmons Sisters, Tragi-Comic Chanteuses.* Bradby, tense as a board, looked about.

'Are we going straight to the manager's office?' He asked, to which Sam shook his head.

'It's Coates I need to see.'

They moved past the wings and found the stage manager's cubby-hole, but it was empty. A stagehand then appeared, looking suspicious, and asked what it was they wanted - whereupon recognition broke.

'I remember you,' Bradby said, eying him keenly. 'We last spoke underneath the stage, didn't we? When our electro-magnet had to be moved? My guvnor gave you a tip.'

'Oh, yes…' looking uncertain, the man faced Sam. 'What can I do for you, sir?'

'We're here to see Mr Coates,' Sam told him. 'It's business.'

'Business?' A sceptical look appeared. 'After what happened with the ape trick? I doubt if anyone wants to talk business with you just now, mister-'

'I'll see Coates,' Sam interrupted, leaning forward. Beside him, Bradby grunted.

'He's busy,' came the quick reply. The man was growing nervous, his eyes darting about. From the stage, two female voices rose in deafening crescendo.

'But you can fetch him,' Sam said. 'If you do, there might be a drink in it for you. If you don't-'

'If you don't, I'll be waiting outside,' Bradby finished.

'All right… no need for that.' Taking a step back, the other raised both hands. 'I'll tell him… but it's best you find a quiet spot, isn't it? I mean, not here…'

'Why not under the stage?' Sam said. 'It's as good as anywhere else, is it not?'

The stagehand nodded and began to move – whereupon Bradby seized his arm.

'We'll wait ten minutes,' he said, pushing his face close. 'And if Coates hasn't come down by then, I'll come looking for you. Clear enough?'

With a gulp, the fellow went off swiftly.

They had no need to wait ten minutes, nor even five. A short time after they had descended to the gloomy, dusty under-stage, footsteps sounded on the steps and Jack Coates appeared, looking very wary indeed. Above him another figure loomed, but did not descend.

'My insurance,' Coates said, jerking his thumb over his shoulder. 'Just in case.'

'In case of what?' Sam took a pace forward. 'Were you expecting trouble?'

The stage manager hesitated, glancing past him to where Bradby stood with arms folded. They had found a gas jet and lit it, casting a lurid glow over the cramped space. Overhead, the Simmons Sisters clumped about on the boards.

'I wasn't sure what to expect,' Coates answered. 'And this is untoward, Mr Vasey. Your father caused us a lot of difficulties when he last played here - not to say considerable expense. You know what I'm referring to, of course.'

'You're referring to the night our assistant Nancy Poole was murdered, you mean,' Sam said, speaking low. 'We're not likely to have forgotten that.'

Coates tensed, throwing a glance towards the stairway The burly figure of one of his roustabouts was clearly visible, seated on the top step.

'Of course - a terrible event,' he said quickly. 'I hope and pray this vile murderer is caught, just as everyone else does.'

'But you were thinking of what went before,' Sam told him. 'When she disappeared backstage – just popping outside, she said. Only, she never came back. Nor did the young man who was playing the ape – his name's Arthur. Bit of a rogue, that one, wouldn't you say? A Jack-the-Lad?'

'I've no idea,' Coates retorted. 'You brought him here…'

'Nancy brought him,' Sam said. 'Though she'd never spoken of him before. Perhaps he was recommended – or even forced upon her. What do you think?'

'Me? How would I know?'

Coates was frowning now, glancing from one to the other. But Sam was thinking fast, running over the events since he had last stood beside the man in the wings of this Hall, and seen the ape trick ruined. Coates had seemed as shocked as he was at the time, but…

'You'll have heard about our trouble… The Great Albertini's trouble, I mean,' he went on. 'A nasty little campaign to bring us low - if not to put us out of business entirely. We think it was arranged by Lysander Hobbs. Have you seen him lately?'

'No, I haven't,' Coates answered. 'And this is sounding worse by the minute…' he swallowed, his frown deepening. 'I came down here in good faith, Vasey, thinking maybe you wanted to apologise for what happened on my stage, in private. Now you start making accusations… you'd better leave. I've got things to do-'

'I think you came down here because it's private, right enough,' Sam broke in. 'You wouldn't want anyone overhearing any of this, would you? Like your manager, for instance. Does he know you've been taking bribes from Hobbs?'

It was a stab in the dark, he knew – even reckless, but he was tired of being fobbed off. He trusted John Chambers, and had taken him at his word. This weaselly little man was hiding something, he was sure – and quite soon, he was proved right.

'That's a lie!' Coates jerked as if struck. 'I wouldn't… you've no right! Get out of here now, or I'll-'

'What, call your chum down? Well, why not do it? I fancy a bout here and now… got a bit of anger to work off, you see.'

It was Bradby, moving slowly towards Coates with a look that would brook no argument. Sam's instinct was to restrain him, but he did not. He merely summoned a grim smile, raised his hand and pointed a finger.

'You don't really want anyone else to hear this, do you?' He demanded. 'What with Nancy's death following only hours after she and Arthur wrecked the ape trick? Even Hobbs is afraid, we hear. His people are fleeing like rabbits - and it was more than a terrible event, as you put it. We're speaking of murder - surely you don't want to get tangled up in something like that? The police are desperate for witnesses, I hear…'

He broke off, as there came a gruff voice from the stairway: the big man was on his feet, taking a step down. 'Is everything all right, Mister Coates?' He called.

A moment passed, in which the three men eyed each other: Sam wearing an expression of polite enquiry, Bradby one of belligerence, Coates now so anxious that he was starting to sweat. He faltered, his tongue flew out to wet his lips… then he half-turned, and called out in reply.

'All's well… just business talk. No need for you to hang around.'

The stagehand hesitated, peering downwards. But when Coates lifted a hand in casual dismissal, he turned to go. A door closed, whereupon the stage manager faced his interrogators again… and to their surprise, his spirits seemed to sink. He swallowed again - and when he spoke at last, his voice was hoarse.

'For God's sake, let this go no further,' he muttered. 'I'll tell you what I know – but no more talk of murder!' His frightened eyes were on Sam's. 'What I earn in this place wouldn't keep a pauper's family,' he added. 'Who wouldn't want more? But I went no further than I was bidden – and I know nothing about what happened to Nancy Poole. I'll swear that on my children's lives – all nine of them! D'you see now?'

'I might,' Sam replied after a moment; he was about to get some answers at last, and though he maintained a severe look, his overwhelming sense was one of relief.

'So – you talk, and I'll listen,' he added. 'Is that not fair enough?'

FIFTEEN

In the end, it was more like a confession than a revelation. And when it was over, the scrawny little stage manager of the Star Music Hall appeared almost glad to have unburdened himself. He was not built for real skullduggery: that was how Bradby would assess the man's character later. For now, while The Star's orchestra played, and the Simmons Sisters left the stage to make way for another act, he and Sam merely listened.

'I've known Hobbs a long time,' Coates said, avoiding their eyes. 'Never liked him, but he did me a few favours, which I repaid. Didn't think I'd see much of him again, when he went to America. But after he got back he called me to him, made a proposition. I couldn't refuse – any more than others could, who needed his money. Like Cuddy Carter with his gambling… only he was too much of a liability. Hobbs gave up on him.'

He broke off, looking away. He was sitting on the bottom step, the other two gazing down at him. When they merely waited, he glanced up and resumed.

'I've nothing against your father – I swear it,' he said to Sam. 'But this business is… well, I've no need to tell you. Hobbs had his reasons: a notion to make Albert Vasey take second place to him or something - I didn't ask. I just called in a few favours of my own… people who would do what was wanted, take their money and keep quiet.'

'Like Fred Bowes?' Sam asked.

'Well… as it happens, yes.' Coates looked startled. 'I knew him from Gatti's…'

'What about his nephew?' Sam persisted. 'Billy, that is, who worked at The Tivoli.'

'I don't know him,' the other answered, shaking his head. 'There were others doing mischief for Hobbs. That trouble you had at the Daisy-Cup, when your magic walnut trick failed, was one piece. The mind-reading business was supposed to be a taste – and your girl Nancy was part of it. But I suppose you know that now?'

Neither Sam nor Bradby answered, merely stared until he spoke again.

'As for what happened here, with the ape trick…' Coates gave a shrug. 'Nancy brought that young rogue in, only I doubt if it was her choice.'

He paused, and Sam's eyes narrowed. 'Go on,' he said.

'It all changed, you see,' Coates said, with a frown. 'After Brunner was killed, I mean… it wasn't Hobbs's doing, I'd bet on that. Then, when the Chinaman got shot…' he shook his head. 'Someone else was at work, doing things no-one bargained for… some gang, settling scores maybe. It scared me stiff, for one.'

Sam felt Bradby's eyes on him, but kept his on Coates. The two of them knew only too well about the 'gang' who had done murder – and what sort of scores they were settling.

'Tell me about the ape trick, then,' Sam said, calmly enough. 'How far were you involved in what happened here?'

Coates hesitated, then: 'I knew something was up, but she wouldn't say exactly what… Nancy, that is. We – me and my boys - we had to let things take their course and not interfere - like letting the one in the ape suit go, when he legged it for the stage door. That way, we'd all look well shocked after it went wrong…' he met Sam's eye briefly. 'That Arthur, he's a wrong 'un – whoever he was working for,' he added, with distaste. 'Maybe you need to work it all out.'

'I will,' Sam said. 'But just now, I want to hear what you think.'

'What I think?' Coates echoed. 'I think Nancy was in deeper than she wanted to be, or meaned to be… she went from working for Hobbs to something else. Maybe someone got to her, scared the life out of her and told her what to do, or else. So, as you said, Arthur – if that's really his name – was forced on her… someone she never asked for.' He dropped his gaze. 'What they cooked up between them, I don't know. But it killed your father's act stone dead, didn't it?'

He gave a start, aware of what he had just said: it was not only The Great Albertini's act that had been killed that night. Seeing the looks that came over the faces of Sam and Bradby, he sought to soften the blow

'I didn't mean… look - I'm as in the dark as you are, about that night,' he blurted. 'Hobbs wanted to wreck the ape business – a last straw, so to speak. But I told you I don't believe he would have used Arthur, and that's the truth. So…' he spread his hands. 'That's all I know,' he added. 'I'm done.'

From overhead came a flourish from the orchestra, followed by a burst of applause. Sam eyed Bradby, who shook his head; they had learned all they would here. And though he still looked angry enough to deal out retribution to their informant, it was not about to happen.

Without a word, Sam gestured to Coates to vacate the stairway, which he did at once, stepping back quickly. But when the other two brushed past him and began to climb the steps, he let out a breath of relief. Sam glanced back once, to see the man's forehead sheened with sweat, glistening in the gaslight.

***

When they returned to Highgate that evening, a surprise awaited.

In the parlour, nursing a glass of port wine, was Mattie Burns. Nearby sat Louise Sidorov, with Albert facing them. As Sam and Bradby came in he stood up, regarded them both, then went to pour whiskeys.

'It looks like a council of war,' Sam said, after he had greeted their unexpected guest.

'Just visiting friends, Sammy,' Mattie said, cheerfully enough.

Beside her, Louise threw Sam a wan smile. 'I have told Mattie everything now. She's kind and brave – as you gentlemen have been. I will no longer keep these secrets from my true friends.'

With a glance from her to Mattie, Sam sank into a chair. Bradby went to Albert, took two glasses from him and brought them over. He sat down beside Sam, whereupon they fortified themselves in silence.

'Well, was it worth the trip?' Albert demanded, with impatience. 'Tell!'

Sam drew a breath and told them. It took less time than he expected, but the reaction was stark: a shocked silence. Finally,

Mattie took a drink and stared around.

'By golly,' she murmured.

The silence returned, only to be broken by Louise Sidorov. 'Well, I have heard enough now,' she said with a sigh. 'You have your own troubles, and I will no longer put you in danger… any of you,' she added, with a glance at Sam. 'I'm the one the Okhrana men seek, and I will leave here tonight.' Seeing him about to speak, she raised a hand.

'Please, hear what I have to say. Mattie has offered to bring me to her flat, and to let me stay there while I make plans to go elsewhere.'

She threw a glance at her friend, who nodded.

'She'll be as safe there as she could be anywhere, Sammy,' she said. 'It's a busy place – good neighbours above and below me. And…' - this with a glance at Albert – 'your pappy has offered to take us, and see us inside. Such a gallant fellow, eh?'

All eyes went to Albert, who looked somewhat embarrassed 'We've discussed it, and we all think it best,' he said to Sam. 'If Mrs Sidorov leaves here late tonight, in disguise – a man's clothing would be best – even if those devils are watching, they aren't likely to recognise her. We'll leave a light burning in her room. Once at Mattie's, she can act freely.'

Somewhat deflated, Sam let out a breath. 'Well, it seems the council of war has already been held without us,' he said, turning to Bradby.

Bradby, however, wore a look of approval. 'I think it's wise – but I won't let you go alone, Guvnor. Let me ready the carriage. Then we'll drive down – somewhere off the Tottenham Court Road, is it not?' He looked to Mattie, who nodded.

'Right in the West End,' she answered. 'It's tiny, but it suits me - and if Louise will squeeze herself in, we'll be comfy enough.'

And all at once, there seemed little left to say. Sam glanced at Louise, who looked away quickly. And soon after, she rose to do her packing. Matty, it transpired, had been to her house and brought clothes and other necessities. After both women had left the room, Sam looked at his father.

'Well, this may be all to the good,' he said, 'but it isn't the end of our business. It seems to me that the last person to see Nancy was Arthur – and I won't let that rest.'

'Nor will I,' Bradby said. 'We need to find him and-'

'But it's for the police to track him down,' Albert interrupted. 'You must tell Drewe what's happened. They've got that older rogue in custody – Gower, who tried to warn you off. If I had my way, he'd be forced to tell them where to find Arthur.'

'I'll speak to Drewe in the morning,' Sam replied. 'But after that, I'm paying another visit to the man who set this business in motion. I'm talking about our difficulties, not Louise's.'

'You mean Hobbs?' Albert was frowning. 'What good would that do? We know what he's been up to, but how would we prove it? Do you think any of those rogues who did his dirty work would admit it? Once our guest has gone, we need to try and put these terrible weeks behind us, and plan our return to performing – don't you agree?'

'And leave Nancy's murder unsolved?' Sam said, meeting his eye. 'No, father. No matter what she did to us, I still can't do that.'

With a look of helplessness, Albert turned to Bradby, but his expression was enough: the two of them were of one mind. With a sigh he sat down, raised his glass and took a drink.

'You're the manager,' he said finally. 'You'd better do what you think best.'

'I will,' Sam replied. 'We'll go and see Hobbs tomorrow. If nothing else, we'll make him feel uncomfortable - won't we?' He turned to Bradby, who nodded.

'We can do that, at least,' he said.

***

To the relief of everyone, the rest of the night passed off according to plan. A little after midnight Louise Sidorov, muffled in a heavy coat and wearing a man's hat, got into the carriage with Mattie. Albert followed close behind with her baggage. Brief farewells followed, Sam seeing them off as Bradby drove smartly out into the avenue. There was no-one about, a light breeze sending leaves swirling as they trotted away into the dark. For a while he stood by the gateway, watching for any sign of movement, but there was nothing. Finally he went back indoors, to find Alice in the hallway.

'I thought you'd gone to bed,' he said.

'I believe I'll miss her after all, Mr Sam,' she said. 'Mrs Sidorov turned out to be a kind lady. She gave me this.' She held out her hand to show him a small, jewelled brooch resting in her palm.

'That was good of her,' he said. 'Then, I suspect she thought you'd earned it.'

The housekeeper nodded. 'I know it's not my place to say this,' she murmured. 'But the lady was sad to leave here… or to leave one of us, anyway. But perhaps you know it already.'

Upon which their eyes met, before she turned and went off towards the kitchen.

***

The morning dawned cold and windy, with a foretaste of the coming winter.

Sam rose early, and after a hurried breakfast went into the office. There he made a telephone call to Sergeant Drewe at Scotland Yard, and gave him a brief account of what had happened since their last meeting. The sergeant was sympathetic, but had no real news; he would tell Inspector Maskell everything when he arrived, he told Sam. He had one new idea to impart, however: in view of the evidence, the fugitive Arthur could at least be charged with theft of an ape costume. It would justify the man's being arrested, so if Sam happened to discover his whereabouts…

With some impatience, he promised to keep the sergeant informed and rang off. Thereafter he sought out Bradby, who had stayed the night after returning from his drive. Louise Sidorov, he reported, was now lodged in Mattie's small flat off the Tottenham Court Road. Albert had insisted on seeing her safely indoors.

'The lady said she'll inform you when she's leaving London,' he told Sam. 'I've a notion she'd like to say a proper goodbye.'

He raised an eyebrow, but Sam was brisk; they should waste no more time. He was eager to beard Hobbs in his den once again – provided he was there. If the man had already closed his office, as Paulo Brunner had claimed, it might prove more difficult.

As it turned out, he need not have worried on that score.

A half hour later, having taken a cab down to the Euston Road, Sam and Bradby walked side by side through the noise and bustle. No-one paid them any mind in the busy street, but a careful observer might have discerned a steely resolve on the faces of both men. In fact Sam had no particular strategy in mind, other than to confront the one who had almost ruined The Great Albertini. And yet, he still believed Hobbs knew more than others said he did - and there was the matter of Nancy, and how he had used her; that alone was enough.

They arrived at the outer door of the building and found it locked, but knocked anyway – several times, and loudly. Whereupon, stepping back on to the pavement, Bradby looked up and believed he saw movement at a window.

'It may be his clerk,' Sam said.

'Well, there's one way to find out.' And he would have put his shoulder to the door there and then, had Sam not stayed him.

'Not that,' he said. 'I won't break the law for Hobbs.' He seized the door-knocker and banged it again, but still nobody came.

'How long are you prepared to wait?' Bradby enquired. 'If you know where he lives…' He broke off as Sam bent down, lifted the brass lid of the letter-box and put his mouth to it.

'We're here to see Hobbs!' he called. 'If you won't answer this door, I'll fetch the police!'

'What are you going to accuse him of?' Bradby wanted to know. 'If you'd told me, I could have borrowed a constable's uniform from somewhere, acted the part.'

They waited a moment longer. Then, just as Bradby was about to air some further suggestion, there came the scrape of a bolt being drawn. Both of them stiffened as the door opened a short way, to reveal the anxious face of the young man who had last admitted Sam and Albert. It was twelve days ago; and in that time, things had changed considerably.

'Mr Hobbs isn't here,' the clerk said at once. 'The agency is closed, and that's all I-'

'You're lying, son.'

Bradby snapped the words out, making the other blink. And even as he opened his mouth to protest, Sam saw that it was true.

'That's unwise of you,' he said, seizing the edge of the door. 'My business won't wait. And I meant what I said: let me in or I'll summon the police.'

'But I can't,' the clerk protested. 'I'm sorry… we're busy, and I have instructions-'

He flinched as Bradby placed his foot in the doorway. 'Best stand aside, lad,' he said mildly. 'I'm a clumsy bastard, so don't make me knock you over.'

A moment followed, but seeing that he was no match for these two, the young man fell back. As he did so, he turned to the stairs behind him and shouted.

'They're coming up! I tried to stop them… coming up now!'

'There's no need to announce us,' Sam said, pushing past him. 'I expect he knows.'

He and Bradby mounted the stairs swiftly, leaving Hobbs' hapless servant below. With Sam leading the way they reached the landing, gained the door to the main office, threw it open and stepped inside – to stop abruptly.

Lysander Hobbs was standing in the middle of the room, levelling a heavy revolver at them with a somewhat unsteady hand.

'Dear oh dear,' Bradby said, after a moment. 'That's not much of a welcome, is it?'

'No, it isn't,' Sam agreed, surveying the big man without expression. Hobbs looked tired, he thought; his face was flushed, his eyes darting between the two of them.

'Get out, Vasey,' he said, his voice hoarse. 'You're trespassing.'

'Why not call the police, then?' Sam suggested. He pointed to the man's telephone. His desk was an untidy mass of papers and ledgers.

'I've nothing to say to you,' Hobbs retorted. 'And I'm very busy, so-'

'So we heard,' Sam broke in. 'Not going out of business,

surely? You, who could buy my father out any time, so you said?'

'What do you want?' The big man was breathing hard, his broad chest rising rapidly. 'Compensation, is it? Or just revenge?'

'How about justice?' Sam took a step forward. 'For Nancy Poole.'

Hobbs flinched, but said nothing.

'You won't use that – *sir*,' Bradby said then, with a contemptuous gesture towards the gun. 'It seems to me you're in enough hot water already, don't you think?'

'To hell with you,' the other retorted. 'You can't come here talking to me like that-'

'Mr Hobbs.' In an icy tone, Sam cut him short. 'Mr Durrell is right: you're already in trouble, and I think you know it.' He nodded towards the cluttered desk. 'I heard you were shutting up shop – why is that?'

'I've done no wrong!' Hobbs blurted out. 'I'm a man of business…' But with a nervous cough, he trailed off.

'You look like you need a drink,' Sam said. 'Why not put the gun down, and take a bracer?'

There followed a moment, in which Hobbs wavered. He glanced towards the door, but there was no sign of his assistant. Coming to a decision, he backed towards his desk and placed the gun down upon it.

'I asked if you wanted compensation,' he said, trying to master the situation. 'Can we not talk like men of the world, and reach an accommodation of some kind?'

'You can't put a price on a young woman's life,' Bradby said, letting his anger show. But at a glance from Sam, he lowered his gaze.

'An accommodation? It would depend on what you tell me,' Sam said, eying Hobbs keenly. 'You read the newspapers, so you'll know there's a hunt for a murderer going on. A young villain who calls himself Arthur might be a suspect. Do you know him?'

'No, I don't,' Hobbs replied at once. But he was avoiding Sam's eye. Nervously, he edged around his desk to the table where decanters and glasses stood, and poured himself a drink.

'Careful, sir,' Bradby said. 'You're looking a bit shaky.'

The man took a gulp, lowered the glass and turned to them. He was summoning some words of response, but once again Sam cut him short.

'Let's not waste time,' he said. 'We both know what you did to my father's act, arranging mishaps and everything. The last one was the most spectacular, wasn't it – the ape that disappeared for good, along with the assistant? That same night, she was found dead – strangled. And you claim you don't know the man I speak of?'

'I don't know him,' Hobbs insisted. 'And I've nothing to do with any murder – of jugglers or of anyone else! As for Miss Poole, her involvement with me was…'

'Strictly a business arrangement?' Sam suggested, stepping closer. Behind him, he heard Bradby mutter under his breath.

'And why not?' Hobbs threw back angrily. 'You think I'm the only one in London who makes such deals? Fair competition is-'

'Fair?' Sam snapped, raising a finger to point. 'You blackmailed Nancy… you knew about her private life, and scared her into thinking she could lose her place if you spread the word. So she agreed to spike our act – my father's phrase, you'll recall.' And when Hobbs seemed lost for an answer, he pressed his advantage. 'But things went askew, didn't they? I should tell you that I've had an interesting talk with Jack Coates, down at The Star in Bermondsey. Names were banded about – yours among them. Moreover, perhaps you're not aware that the police have made an arrest: an old villain called Gower who held me at gunpoint – like you just tried to do. His accomplice was this same Arthur I've mentioned, and you still claim you don't know him?' He gave a snort. 'Maybe you should try telling it to Inspector Maskell at Scotland Yard. He's mighty keen to make another arrest – and after all that's happened, I don't think he's too fussy who it is-'

'Enough, damn you!'

Hobbs's shout was almost a roar, of rage mingled with fear. Watched by the other two, he put the glass to his mouth, drained its contents and threw it violently against the wall, where it shattered into fragments. Whereupon, breathing hard, he turned upon his inquisitor.

'I never wanted that blasted young fool involved!' He cried. 'I use people I can trust, or who owe me - and yes, Alf Gower was one,' he added. 'He's never failed me over the years. So when he wanted to bring his boy in I agreed – bloody fool that I was. And now…' Hobbs coughed again, and while Sam and Bradby watched, he lurched to his chair and sank down heavily.

'The man you want may call himself Arthur,' he went on, 'but his real name's Charlie Gower. He's Alf Gower's son - and whoever he's really working for, I swear it isn't me!'

Whereupon he looked up, and met Sam's gaze warily.

'So,' he said, with a sigh. 'What do you intend to do now? Tell me, and let's get it over with!'

SIXTEEN

It wasn't pleasant listening, but it was clear enough. While Sam stood over him with Bradby close by, Lysander Hobbs told what he was prepared to tell, and no more.

When Nancy had learned that The Great Albertini was reviving his disappearing ape trick and told Hobbs, the man admitted, he knew what to do and which man to use: Alfred Gower. Past his best years he may have been, but he was capable of playing the ape - or so Hobbs thought. Except that Gower had refused, and instead brought his son in to take his place. What followed was known only too well to the Albertini company.

'I won't defend that little ferret,' Hobbs said caustically. 'But I trusted Alf to keep him in order - and I don't know anything about them holding you at gunpoint. Charlie Gower was paid to mess up the trick – Nancy told him how. After that, he was to make himself scarce. Whatever happened afterwards I don't know, and I'll swear until doomsday I know nothing about her murder. I'll say the same to the police – let them prove different!'

He fell silent, lowering his eyes to the papers on his desk. Sam exchanged looks with Bradby, then allowed his glance to stray across the room; the photograph of the Great Albertini was still in its place on the wall.

'Was it really that important to you?' He asked finally, looking hard at his father's old rival. 'To ruin Albert, whom you once admired? You're a wealthy man - doing better as an agent than you ever did as a conjuror, they say. Was it still not enough?'

'As I said, it was business,' Hobbs answered shortly.

'So you did,' Sam replied. 'And you asked what I intend to do now. Well…' he paused, then: 'Perhaps we can make one of those deals you spoke of, after all...'

'Just one minute, Mr Sam.'

He turned, to see Bradby frowning at him.

'This man could be an accessory,' he added. 'Employing the Gowers, I mean. He should own up. There's corruption in what he's done, isn't there?'

'Perhaps there is,' Sam nodded. 'But for now, I think Mr Hobbs can help us to young Arthur – Charlie, I should say. After that one's been arrested, I might put in a good word for you with the police… what do you think?'

The question was for Hobbs, who looked uncertain now. He threw a glance at Bradby, then turned quickly to Sam. 'I… I might be prepared to co-operate,' he said, and cleared his throat. 'But I can't be sure where Charlie Gower is. Hasn't his old man talked?'

Bradby gave a grunt of contempt. 'What, informed on his own son?' He growled. 'Why should he do that - would you? No… likely you would,' he added.

Sam was regarding Hobbs steadily. 'You'll know where he lives – or used to live,' he said. 'Give me the address, and that of any other place he might be. Then we'll leave you. But play false, and I'll tell tales to the police. I might even exaggerate a bit – or if I don't, my father will. You can guess how he feels about you, just now.'

He stopped… whereupon Bradby gave a sigh, and turned to go.

'I'll wait downstairs,' he said. 'But don't worry if he makes a grab for the gun.' He gestured to the weapon where it lay. 'That's old army issue,' he said to Hobbs. 'Hard to get ammunition for them these days, since they brought Webleys into service. Someone's sold you a pup.'

He walked to the door and went out, leaving it ajar. But Sam fixed Hobbs with an expectant look, and waited.

***

Late that afternoon, a horse-drawn police van turned off Farringdon Street, near the Holborn Viaduct, and drew up in a narrow side-street. Behind it, as passers-by stopped to stare, a hansom pulled up. When several policemen emerged from the van, Sam and Bradby descended from the cab and joined them. They were led by a tall figure in hat and coat.

'I'll remind you that, as long as you're here, you're under my orders,' Inspector Maskell said to Sam. 'You are witnesses, but you have no authority - let alone powers of arrest.'

Both he and Bradby nodded, their eyes straying to the opening of a narrow lane: an alleyway of old terraced houses, dowdy and crumbling. Here, according to Lysander Hobbs, was the home of Alfred Gower: a one-time costermonger who did a little housebreaking on the side. The man's wife was long gone, but the son was believed to use the house. To Sam's thinking, it was unlikely they would find him here – but having searched other premises without result, Maskell was almost desperate.

'Clear the street!' The inspector's order to his constables was terse. As they hurried to obey, he threw a look at Sam.'You and your man stand well back, Vasey. And in case you're interested, I'm still displeased at you taking matters into your own hands as you've done. I'll want sworn depositions from you, at the very least.'

'Very well,' Sam replied. 'If you think it helps.'

The other turned as his men moved swiftly, ordering bystanders away and forming a cordon across the entrance to the alley, which was a cul-de-sac. When the way was clear, with just a barking dog defying them, they waited for Maskell to lead them forward. Their target was the third house on the left, with a boarded-up front window. Soon they had gathered on either side of the door, on which Maskell rapped loudly. The dog barked on lustily.

'If there's a rear way out, he'll be through it before they've broken the door in,' Bradby observed drily. 'I hope they've put a man back there.'

Sam was watching the house, his eyes straying to the upper storey. The roof was in poor condition, with slates missing. Rain would pour in… could Charlie Gower really be inside?

There was a crash, as the constables forced the door. Eagerly they piled into the house, Maskell following. There followed muffled shouts from within, along with a banging of doors. Sam took a few steps forward, with Bradby close behind – then at a sound from above his head, he looked up sharply.

Someone in shirt sleeves was climbing through the roof, knocking slates aside in the process.

'Bloody hell,' Bradby exclaimed. 'Will you look at that?'

'Call Maskell,' Sam said. 'I'll watch where he goes.' And as Bradby moved swiftly to the open doorway he stepped back, squinting upwards. It would be easy enough, he saw, for Charlie Gower – and there was no mistaking him – to get out and make his way along the terraced rooftops. Moreover, Maskell had left only one man by the turning, as a safeguard.

'Up there!' Sam shouted, pointing. The constable looked up, and fumbled for his whistle.

But Gower wasn't about to get caught that easily: Sam knew it, as he watched him get clear of the rafters and clamber unsteadily on to the roof. Broken slates skittered down, to hit the ground with a clatter. The dog ceased barking, yelped and raced off.

'There's no way clear!' Sam shouted, gazing up at the fugitive. 'Give it up!'

His answer was a loud curse as Gower swung himself round, seeking escape. His only possible course seemed to be to make for the end of the blind alley, get to the last house and somehow find a way down. But even as he wavered, constables emerged from the doorway into the street. Maskell followed, with Bradby bringing up the rear. When the inspector looked at him, Sam pointed to the roof.

'Don't lose sight!' Maskell shouted, stepping back to gaze upwards - whereupon realisation hit Sam like a blow.

The houses were back-to-backs. Gower only had to disappear over the dividing ridge, climb down into the next side-street, and he could be away.

Without stopping to think, he ran to the end of the alley, past the stolid constable who was blowing his whistle to no particular purpose, and out into the side-street. Here a small crowd had gathered, chattering excitedly. Sam had to push through them, occasioning some angry ripostes. But once clear, he quickened his pace to the next turning – in time to see a figure slide down a rooftop and jump to the cobbled street, where he landed badly.

In a matter of seconds Sam was upon him. Breathless and dishevelled, his shirt torn and dirty, Gower peered balefully up at him. In his desperate scramble through the roof he had cut himself, streaks of blood showing in several places.

'I told you to give it up,' Sam breathed. 'They're all around you.'

'You can go to blazes!' Was the reply. Painfully he got himself on to all fours, wincing as an ankle pained him. But before he could rise, there were shouts from the end of the street… looking round, he cursed again.

Without looking behind, Sam leaned down and grabbed his arm.

'You walked away from me before,' he said. 'Left your father to his fate, too. I won't let you go this time – but I need an answer before they take you. Did you kill Nancy?'

His answer was a burst of harsh laughter, more like a bark. But when Sam gripped him tightly, the man squirmed.

'Of course I didn't kill her, you bloody clown!' He cried. 'I'd have walked through fire for her! More fool I… she's a woman's woman, didn't you know? Now get off me!'

For a moment Sam looked into Charlie Gower's eyes and saw - what? Fear and hatred… and perhaps something more. Breathing hard, he straightened himself and dropped the man's arm, even as footsteps came running up behind him. Then he was pushed roughly aside as constables seized their quarry, hauling him to his feet. In the melee that followed he stepped away, catching only glimpses of the brash young man who had once played the ape so convincingly, on the stage of The Star Music Hall.

He heard the clink of handcuffs, the angry mutterings of the police who had almost lost their man, before a hand landed on his shoulder. He turned to see Bradby, somewhat out-of-breath, a look of concern on his face.

'I'm all right,' he said. 'It's over.'

'So I see,' Bradby replied, glancing at the constables as they clustered about their prisoner. 'Did he say anything?'

Sam made no answer. His mind whirling, he turned away and, with Bradby beside him, walked to the end of the narrow street. Here they stopped as Inspector Maskell appeared, blocking their way. He was about to speak – but seeing the look on Sam's face, he thought better of it.

***

When evening fell, the Vaseys went to Scotland Yard at Maskell's bidding - to clear up any misunderstandings, he insisted. It was a somewhat fraught meeting, not least because Charlie Gower, it transpired, had sworn vehemently that he was not Nancy's murderer. He would admit to anything else, it seemed, knowing that he faced prison, but on that point he was adamant: he had adored Nancy after meeting her privately through Lysander Hobbs, and had pursued her from the start. And though he was rebuffed, he would rather have died, he insisted, than harm a hair on her head.

'He's a talker, is that one,' Sergeant Drewe said. 'Unlike his old man.'

The four of them sat in Maskell's office, the two detectives facing Sam and his father. Albert had insisted on accompanying Sam, though the business was distasteful to him. But at least everything was in the open now, and since the departure of Louise Sidorov, he had relaxed enough to regain some of his old authority. Maskell, however, was far from content – because once again, there was the maddening fact of an absence of witnesses.

'We can question Charlie Gower until doomsday' he said shortly. 'But he swears he never saw Miss Poole again after he left the Music Hall, and we can't prove otherwise. Nor can we be certain he was the last person to see her. Moreover…' he glanced at his fellow officer. 'To Sergeant Drewe's eyes, the man doesn't have the demeanour of a cold-blooded murderer. I suppose I must bow to his experience in these matters.'

'Just an opinion, sir,' Drewe said stiffly. 'But I've encountered quite a few over the years.'

'Have you asked him who he was working for?' Sam enquired, having mulled it over. 'Lysander Hobbs swore it wasn't him, and I think he was telling the truth. When Gower and his father held me in that stable, they warned me off helping Louise Sidorov. It must mean that those Russians – the Okhrana men - hired them. Who else could it be?'

Maskell bristled. 'I'm aware of that,' he replied. 'And nothing would give me more satisfaction than to pursue and collar the murderers. But whatever the Gowers' connection might be with those people, neither the father nor the son will admit to it.'

'Because they're scared,' Drewe put in. 'They're dealing with men more ruthless than they are. They probably think that, since they failed to get Mrs Sidorov out of your protection to somewhere their paymasters could get at her, they'll pay dearly for it.'

It was a sobering thought. Having recalled his unpleasant confrontation with both the Gowers, Sam spoke up. 'Have you wondered why the Russians would hire a couple of small-time rogues? They knew we were protecting Louise – they were watching the house. They could have seized me themselves, and done a much better job of scaring me off. Why didn't they?'

'Perhaps they don't speak a word of English,' Albert put in, somewhat wryly.

Sergeant Drewe looked up. 'I think that's more than likely. They came over from Paris. They might know French, but they'd need help here - someone who knows the city.'

'We've spoken of this before, sergeant,' Maskell said tersely. 'Naturally they'd need a base for their operation, but beyond that…'

'It's almost three weeks since Brunner was killed,' Sam broke in impatiently. 'So where could they have been hiding for all this time?'

'We asked the Russian Embassy some time ago for a list of their citizens who reside in London,' Drewe said, with a wry look. 'They've yet to respond.'

Nobody had an answer to that. The notion of combing a city the size of London for Russian speakers who might be willing to host a team of assassins, was daunting. Maskell and his sergeant exchanged looks; for now, there seemed little point in continuing the meeting. Until Albert, who had remained uncharacteristically quiet, spoke up.

'Well… there's someone I know, who might have an idea where to look,' he said. And when the officers turned sharply to him, he added: 'Just a notion… an old acquaintance.'

He looked at Sam, who frowned: did his father mean the one

he thought? He was surprised, for it meant stepping back into the past - to his Hoxton past, where he always refused to tread.

'Indeed? And who might this person be?' Maskell enquired.

'I'll not mention names,' Albert replied, looking away.

'What do you mean?' The inspector's hackles rose at once. 'I demand that you explain – otherwise it could amount to your withholding evidence.'

'I don't see how,' was Albert's reply. 'It's but a matter of asking for an opinion… gossip, if you like. I'm trying to aid you,' he added. 'But if you disapprove, perhaps it's time we left you to continue your work. We wish you every success.'

With that he rose from his chair, causing Maskell to rise from his.

'Wait, Mr Vasey,' he snapped. 'You can't simply leave after that. If there's someone - an informer, say, or even one of the criminal classes whom you think might hold information, you must tell us at once.'

'As I said, it's just a notion,' Albert answered, becoming brisk in turn. 'And in any case, there's little use in me giving you a name, for the person I'm thinking of uses several. However…' he looked pointedly at Sam. The other men turned expectantly.

'My father's right, inspector,' he said, after a moment. 'And if he means who I think he means, there's no point in our putting you on to them. Your arrival would be known about before you even got close, and you'd never learn anything.'

With that, he too stood up. But Maskell took a step forward and would have prevented his leaving, had not Sergeant Drewe played the peacemaker once again.

'It's been a long day, sir,' he said, eying the inspector. 'We've made an arrest, and it's greatly to your credit.' He refrained from looking at Sam: all of them knew he had played a leading part in the capture of Charlie Gower. 'Might I suggest that we let these gentlemen go now?' He went on. 'Perhaps they could return in the morning, by which time they'll have had time to reflect on… on what's been said. What do you think?'

For a moment it looked as if the inspector would refuse – but to the relief of all, he relented. With a nod, he lowered his gaze and stood back to let the Vaseys move towards the door, where they collected their coats. But as Sam turned, hat in hand, he found Drewe's eyes upon him, and understood.

The sergeant was giving them an opportunity: to seek out this acquaintance, and to return with information; in effect, he was asking for Sam's help again. Whether Inspector Maskell saw it in quite the same way, he doubted… but if this was how it must be, he was willing.

With brief farewells they parted, Sam and his father making their way out into The Strand. The lights were on, the street lively with traffic. For a moment they stood on the pavement, breathing in the autumn air.

'I'll get us a cab,' Sam said finally. 'Provided we can find one who'll take us where we want to go.' He paused, raising his eyebrows at Albert. 'To find Eliza Brack, I mean. It's her you were thinking of, isn't it?'

Albert gave a nod.

***

They rode in silence while the hansom clattered through roughly-paved streets, where the glare of electric lighting had long given way to the orange glow of old gas lamps. From the Strand they had passed via Kingsway and Holborn to the Grays Inn Road and from there to Clerkenwell, heading north-east. After crossing Goswell Road, the cab rattled its way along Old Street into Shoreditch, then made a left turn into Hoxton Street. Finally, after turning left again into Mintern Street, the driver pulled up abruptly.

'I expect this is as far as he'll go,' Sam said.

They got out, paid the cabman and watched as he plied his whip, wheeling the horse round to the direction from which they had come. Then he was away, moving swiftly. Soon they had walked half-way along Mintern before entering a side-street, poorly-lit and strewn with refuse. Somewhere close by a dog whined, and further off came the noise of an altercation: raised voices giving way to raucous shouting. Sam eyed his father, whose eyes were on the cobbles at his feet. He had no need to look about him: he knew every back street, every alleyway here – and some of the people who lived in them. Though how long it had been since he last stood on this spot, Sam did not know.

'Shall we go in together?' He asked, jerking his head towards a corner some yards away, whence came the unmistakable sounds of revelry. With a nod, Albert moved forward.

The public house was The Spotted Horse: a ramshackle building with grimy windows and a notoriously bad reputation. Among other things, it was a known haunt of the Green Gate Gang, Hoxton's finest collection of petty villains, street urchins and others of ill repute.

A long time ago, one of their number had been a ragged, tousle-haired boy named Albert Vasey, who later moved away and was lost to the community.

As he pushed open the narrow door, stepping into a smoky, gaslit interior, Sam wanted to tell his father that he knew how he felt, and admired him for it. But he kept his silence and entered the place behind Albert, almost gagging at the smell of stale beer and cheap tobacco. When heads turned, his gaze fell upon men in rough working clothes: fustian trousers spattered with paint and plaster, threadbare coats and caps. The Vaseys' good clothing alone was enough to mark them out: as unwelcome toffs, or even as potential victims for some. And yet, no-one approached them. They were merely observed as they moved towards the bar, where a grizzled, grey-bearded barman peered at Albert's fine coat and top hat… and then, recognition dawned.

'By Christ,' he exclaimed. 'I thought you were dead!'

'Hello, Joseph,' Albert said quietly. 'I thought you were, too.'

'How long has it been?' The other asked. 'Twenty years?' Whereupon, noticing Sam for the first time, he blinked in disbelief. 'Don't tell me this is your boy?'

'It is,' Albert nodded. But when Sam offered his hand, the other made no move.

'We'll drink,' Albert said quickly. 'But business first…' he glanced about, peering through the tobacco fumes. 'Is she here tonight? I mean the duchess.'

There was a pause, but Joseph was starting to relax. He stuck his hand out, whereupon Sam, who had lowered his, raised it again and found himself gripped tightly.

'Tonight?' he echoed, with a trace of a smile. 'She's in every night… part of the furniture.' He jerked his head, indicating a corner of the room which was hidden by standing drinkers. 'I'll bring a bottle over,' he added. 'But tread softly… she's a bit shaky these days. The sight of you might set her off.'

Albert touched Sam on the arm and together they moved through the throng, as men grudgingly made way for them. There were a few hostile looks, but finally they came to the gloomy corner where two or three ruffians stood, eying the intruders belligerently. Albert ignored them, however, and approached a small table where sat a tiny figure in a black frock and a wide-brimmed hat trimmed with lace. A jaunty pink flower poked from the hat brim… but it was the face beneath that brought Sam to a halt: gaunt, heavily rouged and powdered, with shiny, bird-like eyes that looked up at once.

'Hello, duchess,' Albert said to the woman, taking off his hat. 'How have you been?'

There was a pause, then a sudden gasp that sent a gout of gin-breath into both their faces.

'Fuck me,' Eliza Brack said. 'Here's the ghost of Al Vasey… what do you want to do, scare me to death?'

SEVENTEEN

Eliza Brack, widow and mother of four sons who were well-known to the police, had once been prominent in the gang named after the Green Gate Inn, Hoxton, following her husband's death at the hands of a rival. Nowadays, it seemed, she had retired from any involvement in questionable activities, but her formidable knowledge was still valued. Hence, after an hour in her company, with Albert buying drinks and tobacco for her pipe, both he and Sam were able to take their leave in possession of two names. The names were of Russian men of advanced years, who dabbled in questionable activities themselves. One was a Jewish tailor named Sadowski, in Canonbury; the other was an old man known as Gregory, or properly Grigori, who kept a lodging-house in Saffron Hill. Beyond those, the duchess claimed, her memory was hazy – but for Albert, it was enough.

'Whatever you might think of her,' he said to Sam as they left The Spotted Horse, 'I'd trust her word, more than I would that of most men. There are rogues and there are villains, but some of them are as straight as a die – unless you have any silver about the house.'

At which their eyes had met, and despite everything, both had started to laugh. It was a release - and it was also, Sam realised, the first time he had seen his father laugh in weeks.

The following morning, he went alone to Scotland Yard to see Inspector Maskell.

This time his greeting was warmer than expected: the inspector had been busy already, it seemed, after Sam had informed him by telephone of the names he and Albert had been given. No sooner had Sam entered the office, than he was telling him that one of the Russians had already been eliminated.

'Sadowski isn't a suspect,' he said quickly. 'We swooped on him at first light, and scared him rigid. Whatever he once did, he's now a harmless old man, looked after by his daughter and her family. Still does a bit of tailoring - but the fact is, he's renounced all connections with the land of his birth. He claims he never speaks Russian, and swears allegiance to Great Britain. We gave him and his wife refuge here, he said, and he's loyal. Mention of the Tsar only angered him.'

'And you're certain he's not playing games?' Sam enquired.

'Sergeant Drewe believed him, and I'm prepared to take his word.'

'So…' Sam took a breath. 'What of this fellow Grigori, in Saffron Hill?'

'Ah, yes… him.' Maskell assumed a thin smile: probably the first time, Sam guessed, that he had seen the man without a look of disapproval. 'Would you care to sit down?'

Sam took a seat while the other began to pace about, as seemed to be his habit.

'We've set a watch on the man's residence,' he said. 'Sergeant Drewe is there now. It looks innocent enough: a shabby lodging-house, for single men. Grigori himself seldom goes out, it seems. But we've made enquiries already - he's a sly one, according to neighbours. Always courteous, but he isn't trusted.'

Sam listened, surprised at the change in Maskell's manner. Until now, the man seemed to have regarded him as little more than a hindrance… had yesterday's capture of Charlie Gower made him revise his opinions?

'Has there been any sign of men who might be your suspects?' He asked.

'Not yet. But according to neighbours, lodgers are in and out all the time.' The inspector gave a brief sigh of impatience. 'The only person who might recognise the one who shot her husband, is Mrs Sidorov.'

'Well, if you brought someone into custody, I think she would be willing to help,' Sam said, though he was by no means certain of it.

'It may come to that,' Maskell said. 'But from what we know…' he hesitated, then met Sam's eye. 'If these men are who we believe they are, and they are indeed hiding in that house, arresting them will be difficult. In short, they're probably under strict orders to carry out their mission whatever the risks

- and not to return until it's completed.'

'Do or die,' Sam remarked, to which the other made no reply.

So: there it was, he thought, and he didn't envy Maskell and his men their task. He recalled Carl Brunner: a good man, brutally killed in error; he thought of the courageous Danya Sidorov, a fine performer who had spoken against tyranny and been pursued across half a continent to London, only to be shot dead in the street in front of his wife. Finally he thought of the woman herself, and felt a sudden pang of regret that he might not see her again…

He glanced up to see Maskell regarding him, somewhat curiously.

'I may have misjudged you, Mr Vasey,' he said. 'I thought you presumptuous – a chip off your father's block. But you have proved yourself to be a considerable asset to us - and if I may say so, a man who cares about justice.'

Blank-faced, Sam could only return the man's gaze, then:

'Which is why I thought to invite you to accompany us, tonight,' the inspector added. 'Purely as a witness, of course… an interested party, if you will. It occurred to my sergeant and I that you would like to be on hand when we storm the citadel, so to speak.'

At that, Sam blinked; this was the last thing he had expected.

'I haven't forgotten the brutal murder of your assistant, Miss Poole,' Maskell said, after a moment. 'If, for the present, we can believe that Charlie Gower was not her murderer, then we must consider who else might have had a motive. Do you follow?'

'I suppose I do,' Sam said, not liking the thought. 'Though I can't believe she was working for those who killed Brunner and Sidorov…'

'Unless she had no choice,' Maskell finished. 'You recall what her friend Miss Willens said – of how she became frightened towards the end? After all, she connived with Charlie Gower to ruin your father's act under Hobbs's orders – did the Russians know that? If so, in their eyes perhaps, like Mrs Sidorov, she posed a risk. We've seen how determined they are to remove any trace – and how ready they are to threaten the lives of women.'

Sam was frowning. 'I'm no longer sure what to think,' he admitted. 'But I'm obliged to you, and I'll go to Saffron Hill. Can I bring Bradby Durrell along too?'

After a moment the other nodded. 'But of course, as was the case yesterday, I'll ask you to stay clear of police activity.'

Sam agreed. And soon afterwards he rose to take his leave, with a new sense of purpose.

***

The night came swiftly, hurried on by heavy rain clouds that burst over the capital around nine o'clock. In the teeming downpour, the police assembled in the shelter of Spitalfields Market, a short distance from Saffron Hill. Sam and Bradby, clad in their ulsters, stood aside while Inspector Maskell instructed his cohort of constables. After a while, Sergeant Drewe walked over to join them.

'We're armed and ready,' he said. 'In fact, my lads are spoiling for a fight – as is the inspector. We've been led up the garden path long enough.'

'You're sure the ones you want are in that house?' Sam asked.

'I wasn't, to begin with,' Drewe admitted. 'But I'm more confident now. Been talking to one of the lodgers - and it turns out there are two men staying there, sharing the best room. Others were kicked out, so they could have it all to themselves. Old Grigori even cooks for them sometimes – can't do enough for them, it seems. They never speak to anyone, just come and go at all hours. Everyone knows they're foreigners, without knowing for certain where they're from – but I think we can make a guess.'

Sam threw a glance at Bradby; what they both felt was a growing sense of excitement. The sergeant then left them to return to his men… and a few minutes later, it was time.

It began in a low-key fashion: instead of storming the house, as Sam half-expected, Maskell and his men crossed busy Farringdon Street, then turned cautiously into Saffron Hill, which was all but deserted in the rain. Two were sent to the alley at the rear of the house. Those who had been on watch all day had reported no sign of the suspects.

'It's a good thing I don't own a revolver,' Bradby murmured, as he and Sam walked behind the constables. 'If I thought those men had any part in what happened to Nancy, I'd pull the trigger on principle.'

Sam said nothing. He had spent a restless day, thinking over all that had happened. That evening he had left Albert trying to busy himself in the outhouse, though it was clear his mind was elsewhere. That the two of them were eager to see an end to the turmoil of the last weeks, went unsaid. The last thing his father had done was to warn him against putting himself in any further danger. But Sam had barely listened: he had formed a private resolve that the ruthless assassins who still threatened Louise Sidorov's life, would never be allowed to get near her.

Now he stiffened, suddenly alert: a hush had fallen – almost as if the entire neighbourhood was waiting. Even the nearby street sounds seemed to fade, as Maskell's men closed in about the door of Grigori's house. Dim lights burned behind curtained windows, but the place was quiet. Finally Maskell was at the door and, without knocking, he turned the handle.

It was not locked – why should it be? It was a lodging-house. The next moment the inspector was inside the hallway, his men following quickly behind. Close to the wall of the adjoining house, Sam and Bradby waited. They heard voices from within, but no sounds of violence… and after exchanging a glance, they moved to the open doorway.

In the hall a feeble gas-jet burned, revealing stairs and closed doors on the left. Ahead of them was a half-open door to a back kitchen, whence came voices, while from overhead the clump of heavy boots on floorboards could be heard. Warily, they walked into the hallway…

Then, like a thunder-crack, came the loud report of a gunshot.

The two of them froze, as the shot was followed immediately by cries and thuds. A second later the kitchen door flew open and Drewe appeared, his face taut. Stepping back smartly, Sam and Bradby let him hurry past them to gain the stairway. As he ran up, two steps at a time, a constable appeared from the kitchen.

'Will you come in here, sirs, and guard the old man?' He asked quickly. 'He's harmless enough – and I'm needed.'

At once Sam nodded, allowing him to sprint up the stairs after his sergeant. From above came more banging, mingled with harsh shouts; the very walls seemed to shake. Then, from the front of the house, came a crash of splintering glass. Swiftly he and Bradby moved into the kitchen - and stopped.

Sitting calmly at a table, a white-haired figure in shirt sleeves and waistcoat was looking at them through a pair of thick pebbled spectacles.

'Good evening, sirs,' the old man said, speaking with a heavy accent. 'Are you wanting accommodation?'

***

What followed was unexpected. It was a brazen display of pained innocence, Bradby would say later, or perhaps merely an act of defiance. Grigori Volkov - émigré, widower and keeper of a cheap lodging-house for single men - knew nothing about his Russian guests, he claimed. And nothing anyone said would shake his testimony.

But the worst was over; that much at least, brought relief. Two men had been taken after a fearful struggle, in which one had fired a revolver when the police burst into their room, badly wounding one of the constables. The other had smashed a window and attempted to flee, before being overpowered. While the injured policeman was hurried away, the prisoners had been handcuffed and forced outside into the rain while their room was searched. Whereupon, to Inspector Maskell's grim satisfaction, what came to light was evidence enough: ammunition, papers printed in Cyrillic script, French francs and a small icon: a gold-haloed figure that was identified as a Russian saint.

Now they were gone, taken outside under close guard. Meanwhile, frightened lodgers who had kept to their rooms during the debacle were allowed to emerge, to be assured that they were now safe.

And despite everything, Grigori too seemed to consider himself safe.

He sat very still at his table, with a half-empty cup of black tea before him. There was a constable on the door, but the others went off to their duties. Meanwhile, Maskell and Drewe stood looking down on their charge, with Sam and Bradby permitted to remain nearby. Understanding how they must feel, the inspector hadn't the heart to exclude them.

'Three weeks, at least, those men have spent under your roof,' the inspector said, eying Grigori coolly. 'Fellow-countrymen of yours, who seem to speak no English, yet you claim you barely know them. Do you expect me to believe that?'

'But why should you not, sir?' The old man replied, with raised eyebrows. 'People of many nations seek a bed here… they are ships that pass. I ask no names, provided they pay.'

'And did they pay?' Maskell enquired. 'In what currency?'

'Shillings, of course.'

'They seem to have received special treatment, don't they?' Sergeant Drewe said. 'Do you normally cook for your lodgers?'

'Sometimes… if they have the money.'

'The matter is,' the inspector said, as if he hadn't heard, 'harbouring violent criminals is a serious offence, carrying a prison sentence. Do you think you could survive such an ordeal, with hard labour? I speak of the treadmill, that breaks men far younger than you.'

The other gave no answer.

'Or, there could be a charge of accessory to murder,' Maskell went on. 'That's a capital offence – I speak of hanging. We don't do it in public any more, of course, but the outcome is the same.'

For the first time, an expression of uncertainty flickered across the old man's face. 'Even if I had done a crime,' he said, his voice rising, 'you cannot take me. I'm Russian citizen…'

'I should have explained,' the inspector broke in tersely. 'The Russian Embassy has denied all knowledge of your friends. They face British justice – and so will you, I'm certain.'

'But this is wrong,' Grigori said, with a trace of agitation. 'I'm innocent man.'

'You're in it up to your scrawny neck, you old skate!'

In consternation the others looked round at Bradby, who could contain himself no longer. Knowing that he was keeping his temper with difficulty, Sam had been on the point of suggesting they leave, but he was too late. Before he could restrain him,

Bradby had taken a step towards the table, making the old man flinch. He looked up, saw the anger directed at him - and perhaps fearing the worst, began to babble.

'You don't understand,' he muttered, his accent growing thicker as he spoke. 'I don't ask what these men do, and they don't tell. Yes, they are Russian… they have business in London. You ask them – I interpret if you wish, and they'll tell the same. I swear on my mother's life, I'm not accessory!'

A moment passed in which, at a forbidding look from Maskell, Bradby stepped back with a muttered apology. Drewe, however, threw him a glance that was far from disapproving. In fact, he seemed to be implying, the threat of violence had broken an impasse. Knowing how he would have been interrogated in his own country, why should Grigori not expect something similar from these men?

'Let me assist you,' Inspector Maskell said at last. 'Let's assume you were forced to co-operate, at personal risk to yourself… might that be nearer the mark?'

All eyes were upon the old man, who looked down suddenly. Taking up his cup, the contents of which must have been stone-cold, he drank quickly. Perhaps it was laced with vodka; the thought occurred absently to Sam as, at last, Maskell's questioning bore fruit.

'They would have killed me,' Grigori said, with a sigh. 'Or beaten me - but you still don't understand. If I informed, I would be killed! You think they won't know what I did?'

'You mean the Okhrana,' the inspector said, after a moment. 'The Tsar's police.'

'They will know!' The old man snapped. 'They don't forgive anyone who disobeys-'

'Are you telling us that you're known to the one who sent those people here?' Drewe broke in. 'That you've assisted his operatives before?'

'No… you see, it's not…' Grigori stumbled nervously over his words. 'I never had choice,' he insisted. 'I have family in Russia… but I'm not criminal! I let these men stay here, do cooking and shopping – no more. You can ask me a thousand times, I will say the same!'

There was brief silence, in which the police officers exchanged looks; it appeared they would get nothing more. But while Bradby stood stiffly beside him, breathing hard, Sam ventured to speak up.

'Do you know that they killed three men?' He enquired, looking hard at Grigori. 'One by design, another because he was a witness, and another simply by mistake. They also intended to kill a woman whose only offence, in their eyes, was to be married to their target. Will you defend such murderers?'

Grigori met his gaze, then looked away quickly.

'Moreover, a friend – one who was almost a sister to me - was murdered too,' Sam went on – at which the other showed sudden anger.

'I don't know this!' He cried, banging his hand on the table so that it shook. 'I tell you I don't ask their business, and-'

'Was it you who found a man to help them – a small-time criminal, say, living not far from here? One who could guide them in London and do their bidding, provided they paid?'

It was a hunch, that flew to Sam's mind that instant. Charlie Gower, he saw, was the link: carrying out sabotage for Lysander Hobbs, while serving the Russians. And how would he have come to their notice, unless someone had recommended him? Grigori had been a petty criminal in his time, and knew the territory… it fitted.

'That's a very good question,' Inspector Maskell said, eying Grigori. 'The one my friend here refers to is named Charlie Gower. Do you know him? Because I can affirm that he knows you. He's in our custody - and talking fast, to save his own neck.'

It was a bluff, of course, but it worked; Sam had to admit that, for once, the inspector had been inspired. Grigori swallowed, looked into his empty teacup, then let out a sigh.

'I know his father,' he admitted. 'Alfred Gower.'

'Of course you do,' Drewe snapped, leaning closer to press the advantage. 'And when you sought him out, he put his boy forward instead.'

The other barely nodded.

'So at last, we have a picture.' Maskell was unable to resist a smile of triumph. 'And I'm arresting you, Volkov... I'm not sure on what charge, but it'll come to me. Now, stand up.'

With that, the inspector signed to the constable on the door to take charge of the prisoner. Sam and Bradby, meanwhile, made their way out.

It was over: the citadel had been stormed, as Maskell had put it, without too much bloodshed. The last Sam saw of the white-haired old Russian, he was getting slowly to his feet, looking somewhat bewildered as he was handcuffed.

Outside, the rain was easing off. They walked into the street – and stopped.

Kneeling on the wet pavement, handcuffed and guarded by three burly constables, were the Okhrana assassins: two heavy-browed, bearded men, who looked up sharply at them. One was badly bruised, glaring at them - likely the man who had tried to escape. The other man... Sam found himself frowning. This one – a born leader - merely stared at him without blinking, his face a blank mask. If he had ever looked into the eyes of a cold-blooded killer, he realised, this was he: a man without scruples, who would have taken his life without pity.

There and then, he savoured relief that such a man was no longer a threat to Louise Sidorov. Taking a breath, he turned his back and walked away.

***

In Farringdon Street they found a cab and, once inside, paused to take stock.

'You know we're not done yet, Mr Sam,' Bradby said, after a while. 'We still don't know who killed Nancy.'

And when Sam turned to him, he went on: 'I never really believed those Russian bastards did it. Once they'd got Mrs Sidorov out of the way, they'd have been off on the first boat to France. They gave no names... no-one got a proper look at them – what would they care? Their orders come from the very top, don't they?'

From outside came the crack of the cabman's whip, as the vehicle lurched into motion. At the familiar rhythm of the horse's hooves, Sam sank back tiredly and shook his head.

Bradby was right; moreover, he realised, the truth had been at the back of his mind all along. Nancy's death was as mysterious as it was bloodily and brutally done – not the work of professionals. Carl Brunner's strangulation had been quick and clean, while the other men had been shot with deadly accuracy.

And besides, he mused, why was she found by Tower Bridge Road, not far from The Star where she had vanished? Surely she would have hailed a cab, made arrangements to get clean away as quickly as possible? He had been too preoccupied with the Gowers, and the Russians, he realised – and yes, with Louise Sidorov too.

He was as much in the dark as he had been ten days ago. What then, was to be done?

EIGHTEEN

The next morning at Highgate, having risen late, Sam sat at the breakfast table in a subdued mood. He was unsure of its cause - after all, a great deal had happened that removed both the imminent danger to Louise Sidorov, and the campaign of sabotage directed at The Great Albertini. There was no reason now why he shouldn't concentrate on the act, as his father was restless to do… apart, of course, from the unsolved murder of Nancy. It weighed on him, even if Albert wanted to put the whole, tragic business behind him. As for the police… he sighed to himself. He had done enough amateur detective work. And though there was the prospect of his being in demand as a witness at some time in the future, he put that aside; when called he would do what was needed, and no more.

When he rose to go to the office the telephone rang, and the caller was Mattie Burns. At once, he remembered that he should have informed her the previous night of the capture of the Okhrana men, which would be a relief to Louise. But it had been late, and he had returned dog-tired… soon he was explaining to Mattie, who was thunderstruck.

'But that's wonderful news!' She exclaimed. 'Tell me all!'

He gave her a brief account of the previous day's events, which then obliged him to tell of the capture of Charlie Gower too. It was an end, he said… a chance for Louise to return to France, without fearing for her life.

Mattie took in the news, then went silent. When Sam asked if she was still there, she said: 'I'd better level with you, Sammy. Louise will be mighty relieved, but it isn't an end. We've talked a good deal since she's been here. From what I've learned, if the boss of those murderers isn't sure they've killed her too, he'll just send someone else to finish the job.'

It was a gloomy thought; Sam remembered that Louise had said the same, before she left the Vasey house. Before he could reply, however, Mattie piped up again.

'Which is why we've come up with a solution between us –

the best one, I'd say. She's coming with me to America.'

'Oh?' Sam was taken aback. 'I'd no idea you were planning to go home.'

'I'm not,' Mattie told him. 'London's my home now, Sammy. But I've been made a good offer, by Huber's in New York. They want me to do my human cannonball act, like I did at the Royal Aquarium, remember?'

'I could hardly forget it,' Sam said. He recalled the spellbinding sight of The Triple-Jointed Terpsichorean Termagant flying from the mouth of the cannon in a puff of smoke, to land in a safety net to thunderous applause. 'So, when do you leave?'

'Next week,' Mattie replied. 'I got that skinflint boss at Huber's to pay my passage – had to twist his arm, mind. But the outcome is, Louise can come as my assistant. Those Russian devils won't find her there - and anyhow, she'll be in disguise.'

'It sounds as if you've got it all worked out. And I'd say Louise is very lucky to have a friend like you.'

'Well - now listen, Sammy.' Mattie adopted a business-like tone. 'There's something you need to think on. You know the promoter, Conrad de Brun? He's putting an American tour together. What with all your troubles, this could be a good chance for Albert, do you see?'

'Yes - I do see,' was Sam's reply.

'If I were you, I'd talk your pappy into it fast. Now I've got to go, things to do… will you come say goodbye, before we leave?'

'I will, Mattie,' Sam said. 'You can count on it.'

Whereupon he ended the call, his mind busy. It was good news, of course - in fact it was a relief: a solution, as Mattie had said. Why, then, was he subdued by it?

***

Albert, however, was unconvinced.

'But there's no need to rush off to America now, don't you see?' He insisted. 'Just look at the newspapers!'

It was clear enough, of course. The capture of the Tivoli Murderers was on every front page, along with the arrest of a man who had been sheltering them: a foreigner of dubious character, it was reported. There were few details about the arrested men. It seemed that every editor had rushed into print to spread the good news: that people could walk the streets of the West End safely again. The villains had been caught with weapons drawn, by constables under the command of Inspector Maskell of the Metropolitan Police, who had kindly supplied a report. One officer was wounded in the struggle, but was recovering in hospital. Meanwhile, speculation that the taking of the assassins had any bearing on the Whitechapel Murders had been discounted: more likely it was a gangland affair, involving money and the settling of scores. Further news would follow…

'Gangs settling scores… that's convenient,' Bradby said dryly, tossing a newspaper down on the table.

It was early afternoon, and The Great Albertini's company had gathered to make plans. While Sam and his props man were still chastened by their recent experience, however, Albert was in a mood of high excitement.

'We must strike while the iron's hot!' he announced. 'Get on to the editors, talk up your part in it: "Mr Sam Vasey, manager of the famous conjuror et cetera et cetera, was on hand at the arrest", and so forth. Give them a statement, saying you're delighted to see the murderers of your good friends, the jugglers Brunner and Chen-Li caught-'

'For pity's sake, father.' Sam cut him off in mid-flow. 'I'll do no such thing. You're forgetting the reason we've been in limbo for the past ten days… or is it longer?'

'Twelve, by my reckoning, since the Halls started cancelling,' Bradby put in. 'After the ape trick went wrong.'

'Of course I haven't forgotten,' Albert retorted. 'But if we put out a story of how I was the victim of professional sabotage, it could work in our favour – surely you see that?'

'I see it,' Sam said, somewhat wearily. 'And likely I could start to line bookings up, now that things have moved on. But to tell you the truth…' he paused, as the notion grew in his mind. 'I think the trip would do us all good – and it would be lucrative. As I said before, we could hire a new Mirabel… try out some new tricks. It makes sense to me, anyway.'

'And to me,' Bradby said. 'If I might be allowed an opinion - Guvnor.'

A moment passed, in which Albert looked at each of them in turn. To Sam's relief, however, he was wavering; seizing the opportunity, he pressed his case.

'Will you at least think about it?' He asked. 'I can arrange a meeting with de Brun, tell him we've got some brand-new illusions to thrill the Americans. He knows you went down well over there last time – why wouldn't he want to include you?'

'Headline you, more like,' Bradby murmured. 'By popular demand, The Great Albertini returns to the USA - come early to avoid disappointment...' He lowered his gaze. 'That's how Nancy would have put it, if she were here,' he added.

'I believe she would,' Sam said.

Albert frowned, and appeared about to utter some riposte… but he didn't.

'Well, then,' he said finally. 'If this were a voting matter, it seems I'd be the loser. Perhaps you need reminding who's the star of the show-'

'And who pays the wages,' Sam broke in. 'Nobody needs reminding. I'm thinking of what's best - for all of us. So…' he drew a breath. 'Will you come with me to see de Brun, and hear what he says? You don't have to accept his offer, if he makes one. What harm can it do?'

With that, he waited. But Bradby caught his eye, throwing him an encouraging glance.

And to the relief of both of them, that afternoon Sam was permitted to arrange a meeting for two days hence, at the office of the Canadian impresario Conrad de Brun.

***

It was Saturday, and the West End was a maelstrom of horse traffic and people. With a lighter step than he had used of late, Sam strode down Shaftesbury Avenue from Cambridge Circus, where he and Albert had alighted from their cab. The two of them then turned into Frith Street, where de Brun's surprisingly small office was located. This man, respected throughout the Music Hall business, had no time for showiness; the contrast with Lysander Hobbs could not have been greater. When they entered, he was almost hidden behind a stack of posters and bills, but soon surfaced to greet them.

'I had the notion you were coming in alone, Sam Vasey,' he drawled in his familiar, measured tones. 'Now, I'm honoured.'

They shook hands, whereupon de Brun cleared a couple of chairs of clutter. Glasses of bourbon appeared, and cigarettes were offered. Sam declined, but The Great Albertini and the well-known promoter were soon puffing at each other over the latter's desk – whereupon it was business from the outset. The man was not known for wasting time.

'I can book you on the Eastern Seaboard tour, for three weeks,' de Brun announced. 'All transportation paid. New York, Philadelphia, Baltimore, and on to Washington. Maybe further south, where it's warmer – more dates to be arranged.'

'Just a moment,' Albert said, taken aback. 'I thought we were here just for an informal discussion.'

'My offer is fifteen thousand dollars a week, for the first two weeks,' was the swift reply. 'After that, you can talk again with my manager over there. Depends on the audiences. But you know the game… were you planning to use the vanishing monkey?'

'The ape.' Sam corrected him mildly. 'No, not this time.'

'That's wise.' Suddenly, de Brun was grinning. 'You might never get it back, eh?'

Albert was drawing on his cigarette, and almost choked. But Sam caught the man's eye, and found his spirits rising. Conrad be Brun had always been a smart operator. And he was not one to let the Albertini Company's recent troubles cloud his judgement.

'You can forget that sorry business,' he said, with a dismissive gesture. 'The Yankees won't know about it… and if your show's as good as I expect it to be, they wouldn't care anyhow.'

'That was my reasoning too,' Sam said approvingly.

'I think you should take up my offer, right now,' de Brun went on, sensing reluctance on Albert's part. 'I've already signed good acts up for the tour. People you'll know - like Florrie Bates, for one.'

'Indeed?' Albert raised his eyebrows. 'I thought she was

doing well enough here.'

'Appearances can deceive,' the other replied. 'She says she needs a change of scene - and between ourselves, maybe the money too.'

'Florrie?' Sam shook his head. 'She's got money to burn – or so I've heard. Never short of work, no family to keep…'

'You sure about that?' de Brun eyed him shrewdly. 'Maybe you don't know her as well as you think.' Whereupon, growing tired of the digression, he spread his hands. 'But getting back to business, Mr Vasey – what do you say? Can I start the ball rolling?'

Deliberately Sam turned to his father: it was his decision, of course. A moment passed, while de Brun waited impassively. Finally, Albert drew a breath and stubbed out his cigarette.

'I'm obliged to you, sir,' he said. 'I wasn't sure what to expect, but you've made it very clear. Can I take a while to think about it?'

'Of course, but not too long,' the promoter answered, straight-faced. 'There are other illusionists, you know.'

'He does know,' Sam said. 'And I promise you a decision, very soon.'

And that was the end of the meeting. A short time after entering the office, Vaseys junior and senior were back in Frith Street, among a throng of people. Not far away, a barrel-organ was churning out a popular song. For a while neither of them spoke until, sensing Sam's disappointment, Albert stopped and turned to him.

'It's natural that I should take time to consider,' he said. 'I didn't expect the matter to be laid out so readily…' he frowned. 'It almost looks as if you and he had discussed it already.'

'Does it?' Sam gave a shrug.

Albert's eyes narrowed. 'It does… and what's this about Florrie Bates being on his tour? She never had any desire to go to America… always said she didn't like Yanks, remember?'

'As it happens, I do,' Sam said, becoming thoughtful. He recalled the last time he had seen Florrie: in the dressing-room at The Star, after she had witnessed the disappearance of Nancy and of Charlie Gower.

'It might be a good idea to have a talk with her,' Albert was saying, as the two of them resumed walking. 'She probably knows de Brun better than we do.'

'Why are you suspicious?' Sam wanted to know. 'The man's as straight as a die – as you once put it. It's a great opportunity he's offering.'

'Perhaps,' Albert allowed.

Whereupon they turned into Shaftesbury Avenue, seeking a cab.

***

Late in the afternoon, Sam sat down in the kitchen to talk to Alice.

'If we do go to America, we'll close the house up like we did last time,' he said. 'You can stay with your sister again, on half-wages for the duration. Would that suit you?'

'It would, Mr Sam,' was her reply. 'I could do with a change. So could you, I expect.'

He had told her of the visit to Conrad de Brun's office, and what might follow. Albert, preoccupied with the decision to be made, had retired to the outhouse.

'As for your father…' Alice gave a sigh. 'If anyone needs to get away for a while, it's him – away from London, and from everyone he knows.'

'He wouldn't quite be leaving everyone behind,' Sam said, and went on to mention Florrie Bates' presence on the tour. For some reason, the woman had been on his mind ever since de Brun had mentioned her.

'You know Bradby's always been a bit sweet on her,' Alice said, after a moment. 'I never understood why. He'd be wasting his time, wouldn't he?'

'I suppose so,' Sam said absently. He was thinking of his conversation with Florrie, in a cab heading towards Lambeth. It seemed like a long time ago…

Then he stiffened, and sat bolt upright.

'Do you mean what I think you mean?' He asked sharply.

'You better ask Mattie Burns, or any of the women you mix with,' Alice replied. 'After what you found out about Nancy…'

She broke off as Sam got to his feet. He started for the door, then checked himself. 'Where's Bradby now?'

Alice mentioned the outhouse – but she had barely uttered the words before he was gone.

***

An hour later he and Bradby were in a cab, bowling across Blackfriars Bridge in the gathering dusk. And Bradby was both surprised and uncomfortable.

'You're being mighty mysterious,' he said. 'It's not like you.'

'I said we're going to pay her a friendly visit,' Sam told him. 'Wish her well, maybe invite her for a drink after her show.' He had made a few telephone calls, and learned that Florrie Bates was due to appear at the Canterbury Music Hall in Lambeth, not far from her home.

'Supposing she's flying off to do another Hall?' Bradby objected. 'She'd be too busy.'

'Then we'll follow.'

'So, what's the hurry?'

For a while Sam gave no answer. He was struggling with a notion that had been brewing, he realised, since the meeting that morning with Conrad de Brun. Finally, he took a breath.

'Have you thought much more about that night at The Star, when everything came crashing down about our ears?' He asked. 'When we lost Nancy?'

'Are you serious?' Bradby turned to him. 'How could I forget?'

'I mean the way it happened,' Sam said. 'Nancy telling Florrie she was stepping out the back - she never did that, during a show. And then Charlie – Arthur, as we knew him – taking off soon after. Florrie said he scared her stiff… do you believe that?'

Bradby frowned, but said nothing.

'I mean, nothing frightens Florrie,' Sam went on. 'And she's seen Albert do the ape trick before – why would that scare her?'

'Would you like to tell me what you're getting at, Mr Sam?' Bradby enquired.

'To be frank, I'm not sure myself,' Sam said. He went on to repeat what Conrad de Brun had said that morning – which made Bradby's frown deepen.

'You think she's hiding something? Because she's a male impersonator, she must be…' he hesitated. 'She must have the same tastes as Nancy did?'

Sam said nothing; things were falling into a pattern that troubled him. Several times he had wondered who the last person was to see Nancy alive – apart from her murderer.

Just then the cab lurched to one side, as the driver turned a corner. Thereafter, the two of them sat in silence until they arrived at the doors of the Canterbury Music Hall, with a noisy crowd outside. Soon they were pushing their way through the throng to the stage door, where a doorman recognised Sam and admitted them both.

Whereupon, having made their way backstage, they received surprising news.

From his vantage-point beside the wings, the Canterbury's stage manager greeted them politely enough, busy as he was. But on learning Sam's business, he shook his head.

'Florrie Bates isn't on tonight, gents. She cancelled, a few days ago. From what I hear she's cancelled all her performances. We can't book her for all the tea in China.'

Sam was silent; so too was Bradby.

'Mind you, I also hear she's off to America soon,' the stage manager added helpfully. 'Too much to do, maybe?' He put on a sly look. 'Perhaps she's got reasons. There's some who find it a useful means of escape for a while, don't they? Those with money troubles, say - like Cuddy Carter. Last I heard, he was in Liverpool…'

He broke off, for Sam was already turning away; he left it to Bradby to thank the man for his information.

Outside, a fog was coming down, the gas-lamps glowing a lurid orange.

'What now?' Bradby asked, looking uneasy. Sam was wound up as tightly as a watch.

'I'm going on to Florrie's,' he replied. 'Just for a chat. Albert thought I should ask her opinion of de Brun and his tours. You don't have to come, if you don't want to.'

'Well, I think maybe I do,' Bradby said.

And soon after, Sam was seeking a cab to take them down to

Kennington Road. They would alight at the turning to a side-street, where Florrie Bates had a small flat.

What would happen after that, should they find her at home, he preferred not to imagine.

NINETEEN

She was at home; but in one way, Sam would think later, he wished she hadn't been.

In a way, he wished she had already left for America - or anywhere, in fact. He wished she had disappeared altogether from his life, from the Music Halls of London – from England, so that he would never have had to see her again. And more than that, he wished with all his heart that she had never been a friend of his: a woman he had liked and respected, who brightened a place when she walked in, as she brightened the stages on which she appeared.

But she was in, answering the door to his knock, Bradby standing beside him. For an instant she looked taken aback, but quickly assumed a broad smile.

'What a lovely surprise! And what brings you to Lambeth – not slumming, I hope?'

'Not exactly, Florrie,' Sam said. 'Call it a social call, along with a bit of business. We… the Company's been offered a chance to join Conrad de Brun's tour, to New York. I hear you're already booked. Could we have a chat?'

'Well…' she hesitated. 'To tell truth, I'm up to my ears in it… packing and such. But you're welcome to come in for a glass of port. It's all I've got.'

'Very kind,' Sam said. When Florrie stepped back from the door, he removed his hat and entered the narrow hallway. Bradby followed.

The flat, they saw, though well-appointed, was in a mess. Boxes and cases were everywhere, some closed up, others open and half-filled. Piles of clothes lay on chairs and couches. A coal fire burned, and the room was too warm. Florrie herself was in a loose gown, her hair pinned up. But she made her way about brightly enough, pouring drinks for her guests. Finding a space, they sat down while she remained standing.

'So, did I hear aright?' She asked. 'Albert's been offered a place on the tour? That's… well, it's rather a coincidence, isn't it?'

Sam watched her, concealing his unease. There was something forced about her manner, which was unlike the woman he knew.

'He's yet to decide whether we go or not,' he said. 'I hope he will, but you know how suspicious he can be. I've told him he can trust de Brun.'

'Of course he can,' Florrie said, with emphasis. 'And yet…' she paused. 'Is it the right time to go, I wonder? For Albert, I mean. After all that's happened, might it look like he's running away – deserting his loyal audience? You know how fickle people are.'

'It might have appeared so, a while back,' Sam allowed. 'But you've heard the news, I'm sure. Now that it's becoming known he was the victim of a dirty campaign by Hobbs-'

'Oh, that awful man!' Florrie broke in. 'I'd like to give him a piece of my mind, the way he treats people.' She raised her fist in a most unladylike manner, and made punching gestures in the air. Bradby, who had been silent since their arrival, tried a grin that didn't quite work.

'You'll have seen the papers too, I expect?' Sam went on. In fact, there was a newspaper on a nearby table, with headlines about the police raid in Saffron Hill. Florrie followed his gaze, and nodded quickly.

'I have… what a turn-up, eh?' She sighed theatrically. 'Seems like yesterday I was watching Brunner perform – Chen-Li too. We can all breathe a little easier now, eh?'

'Well, from what I see the crowds never diminished,' Sam told her. 'Remember that talk you and I had, in a cab? Nothing seems to keep them away. Which is why…' he waited until she met his eye, then added: 'Which is why I was surprised to hear you're heading for the USA just now. You always said it wouldn't suit you.'

'Did I?' Florrie raised her brows. 'Well, you know how it is. Times change…'

'And I hear the money's good,' Bradby put in.

'That's true enough, too,' Florrie agreed.

There was a tautness about her now, which prompted Sam to

press further. While he sought for the words his eyes strayed to the table, where stood a framed photograph of a smiling man in white tie and tails. Again, Florrie followed his gaze.

'My father,' she said quickly. 'He was a singer – a fine baritone.'

'Was he?' Sam put down his glass and rose from the couch. 'May I take a look?' He added, moving towards the table. When Florrie made no objection, he picked up the picture and studied it.

'He's no longer alive, then?' Bradby enquired, to which Florrie signified assent. But at that, Sam turned to catch his eye. Bradby's instinct for sensing a lie seldom failed… and at the swift glance that passed between them, he felt a pang of unease.

'Do you keep his surname?' He asked casually. 'Bates, I mean. Or is it your stage moniker?'

For some reason she was looking uncomfortable. 'Why all the sudden interest in my father?' She asked, somewhat sharply. 'I thought you came to talk about de Brun's American tour… am I wrong?'

'Not entirely,' Sam said quietly. Things could turn unpleasant now, he knew, but…

'The matter is, you mentioned running away, Florrie,' he went on, turning to face her squarely. 'But it looks to me as if it's you who's doing that. I wonder why, when you're so successful? Now I hear the Halls can't book you for all the tea in China. That's how the stage manager at the Canterbury put it. We went there looking for you, but you'd cancelled.'

'And if I did, what business is it of yours, Sam Vasey?'

In a moment, her manner had changed abruptly. Stepping forward, she took her father's photograph from him and set it down. 'Now, much as I'd like to gossip,' she said, looking at each of them in turn, 'I've got a great deal to do. Perhaps we'll have time for a farewell drink before I leave… but I couldn't promise it.'

'Well, that might not be necessary,' Sam replied. 'If we join the tour, we'll have plenty of time together, won't we? On the ship, I mean.' And when she looked down suddenly, he added: 'Or does that notion trouble you?'

'What do you mean by that?' She demanded, raising her head sharply. Her look was one of defiance - and in a moment, he knew precisely where he had seen it before: on the face of Miss Willens, standing with arms folded in the flat she and Nancy had shared.

'Think of all the days we'd have to fill, crossing the Atlantic,' he went on. 'We'll be reminiscing about old times - like when we shared the bill, and Nancy was alive. Plenty of time to talk about Nancy, too… would you like that?'

Florrie drew a breath, but made no answer.

'The fact is, we've never spoken about that night at The Star, have we?' He persisted. 'The night she ruined the ape trick and took off… you were a witness, remember? You told us, in the dressing room. Of course, none of us knew then that you might be one of the last people to see Nancy alive – perhaps the very last, in fact.'

Now, the tension in the room was electric. Florrie drew back from Sam as if stung, putting a hand to her neck and drawing her gown tight. Whereupon Bradby, sitting stiff as a post, gave a cough which made her turn sharply to him.

'You knew more than you told us that night, Miss Bates,' he said quietly. 'Didn't you?'

'What are you saying?' Her words were snapped out. 'Are you accusing me of something? Because if so, you'd better leave now. I won't have it.'

'What could we accuse you of, Florrie?' Sam asked. His face bore no expression, but his heart was sinking fast. Florrie, her chest rising and falling, swung round to face him.

'I won't have it,' she repeated. 'I'm a star! You can't come here upsetting me like this - leave me alone!'

'Perhaps I should have explained,' Sam said. 'My father and I had quite a chat with Conrad de Brun. I was taken aback at the notion you might be short of money – because you are indeed a star. You're one of the highest paid acts on the Halls. I wonder where it all goes?' He looked round deliberately. 'Not on this flat… not in Lambeth.'

There was a moment, in which Florrie appeared lost for words. Briefly, Sam thought she was on the verge of telling him something – but he was mistaken.

'Get out, both of you!' She shouted, with considerable force. 'You've no right! Go!'

'Were you lovers, Miss Bates? You and Nancy?'

Wearing the saddest expression Sam had ever seen on him, Bradby stood up. Startled, she stepped closer to the fire, a sheen of sweat on her brow. Another moment passed, then:

'Her friend – Miss Willens, her name is – told me she thought Nancy was seeing someone secretly,' Sam said. 'A man, she suspected. And a man's cuff-link was found near where she was killed… that wasn't very far from The Star, was it? I might even say, it's between The Star and here.' He paused. 'Was she meeting you that night?'

'Lies! You're a liar!'

It was almost a shriek. Wild-eyed, Florrie darted towards the table – and to the surprise of Sam and Bradby, picked up an object familiar to them: her famous antique walking cane, which she always twirled as part of her act. For a moment, Sam thought she would lash out with it – but he was mistaken.

With a faint scrape of metal, Florrie pulled the cane in two, to reveal a gleaming blade. It was indeed an antique: it was a sword-stick.

'Now get out!' She ordered, levelling the weapon at him. 'Get out – at once!'

The silence that followed was stark. The men exchanged swift glances, but made no move towards the door. Instead, Sam let out a sigh and shook his head.

'Lord above, Florrie,' he breathed. 'Why did you do it? Why did you kill Nancy?'

Her answer was a sharp intake of breath. The short blade - three-sided, and tapering to a deadly point - trembled a little.

'Were you supposed to meet, after she left The Star?' Sam persisted. 'Miss Willens knew Nancy was leaving her… was it for you? Did you plan to run away together? What happened, Florrie? You'd better tell me, because I'm not going away until you do.'

'Nor am I,' Bradby said, his voice taut. 'So, you'd better make up your mind. You can try and use that thing, or…'

'Or we leave and call the police.' Sam finished. 'We'll remain outside until they get here.' He allowed his glance to stray to the sword-stick. 'Is that what you used to kill her?'

He stopped talking and waited. There they stood, in silent tableau: Florrie sweating and trembling, holding the blade unsteadily, Sam and Bradby tense and watchful… until Bradby stepped swiftly towards her, seized her wrist and forced it downwards.

'Best not make things any worse, eh?' He said quietly. With his other hand he gripped the blade, and took it firmly from her. Blood spurted, as Florrie gave a groan and let go. As Bradby threw the weapon across the room, she slumped to the floor and let out a whimper.

'I thought she loved me,' she muttered.

Whereupon she put her face in her hands, and wept piteously.

***

By the time the forces of law arrived - a sergeant from Lambeth Division, along with two constables - the matter had been laid bare. It was a tale of greed and of disappointment – but it was also one of desperation. While they waited for the police, Sam and Bradby heard her admission in silence: Bradby with his hand heavily bandaged, sitting on a couch; Sam on his feet. Seldom had he seen someone brought so low as was Florrie Bates that night: a star of the Halls who had committed a heinous crime, driven by rejection.

'We had such plans,' she muttered, sitting huddled in her gown as if she were cold. 'We kept it secret, of course… even Margaret Willens didn't know. Nancy would have money from Hobbs, I had some savings… she would stay here while we made the final arrangements, then leave for Paris. After that Monte Carlo, Rome, Vienna… the world was ours. No more London smogs, no more flying in the rain between halls… no more drunks shouting from the galleries - and no more being controlled by men!'

She looked up at Sam, red-eyed with weeping. 'One of the highest paid, you said? Am I? You wondered where it all goes… well, I'll tell you. Most of it goes on him!'

She was pointing at the table – more precisely, she was

pointing at the framed photograph of her father. And when both men looked puzzled, she dropped her hand and gave a sigh.

'You'll have passed by him, on your way here,' she said quietly. 'St George's Fields… you know what I'm saying.'

Bradby frowned, not understanding. But Sam glanced again at the photograph, then back to Florrie, and gave a start.

'You mean the Lunatic Asylum?'

'Bethlem Asylum,' Florrie corrected, in a bitter tone. 'He's been there for years… long forgotten. People think he's dead – and he may as well be. Doesn't know what day it is… doesn't even recognise me, his own daughter! I've paid for the best care, but it's no use. He'll die soon, not even remembering he lived. Now, do you begin to see?'

'So… you're leaving others to bury him,' Bradby said. 'Heading off to America-'

'And why should I not?' She threw back angrily. 'You dare to judge me? I've paid for his funeral already – I've put up with more than you'll ever know!'

'But you still haven't answered my question, Florrie,' Sam said quietly. 'What happened to Nancy?'

At that she faltered, her expression one of anguish. But seeing he would persist, she let out a long breath.

'You think you knew her,' she said, with a shake of her head. 'You didn't… not really. You know she came from nothing, but you can't understand how she suffered. Not that she wasn't grateful – to Albert, and to you. You were almost a family to her, in place of the one she tried to forget. The father a drunkard, the mother worn down to nothing, a sister who treated her like dirt. But she could dance – that was her escape. And when you took her on, that was like winning first prize…'

'But it wasn't enough, was it.'

Bradby spoke up, eying her without expression. 'She wanted more… and she found you.'

'No - I found her,' Florrie retorted. 'And I've told you enough.' She looked up angrily. 'You had a bright jewel working for you… Albert had a jewel, but one he never valued enough.'

'Are you talking about money?' Sam felt his own anger rising.

'She was well-paid - and she could have been paid more, had she talked to me. You're wrong: we all valued Nancy – and we trusted her too. I still can't believe she intended to ruin my father - even if she was scared into it. And I still can't understand why you and she-'

'She was backing out!'

Suddenly, Florrie's anguish spilled over. 'Nancy was in turmoil,' she cried. 'She felt terrible after what she'd done. That vile little rat, Charlie Gower – he would have informed on her in an instant. She knew he'd got her in too deep - she thought she had no choice but to run away. Then at the last minute…'

'Yes, now I see it.' Involuntarily Sam took a step forward, to tower over her. 'You were to meet after the show. She waited for you to pick her up, in Tower Bridge Road. But when you arrived, things went wrong. And when she wavered - said she couldn't do it, you lost patience-'

'No… not like that.'

Florrie shook her head. 'She had some wild notion of going back to Margaret Willens, and telling her everything. That woman worshipped her – she would have stood by her, Nancy said. They could have made a plan – but it was madness, and I told her. We stood in the alley like fishwives, screeching at each other - I couldn't bear it. I only meant to strike her, make her see sense-'

'You're lying to us.'

Bradby's words flew out, cutting her short. And when she turned sharply towards him, he too stood up.

'No-one draws a blade like that unless they mean it,' he said. 'Nor do they run their victim through the heart, as you did. Nor rifle her bag afterwards, to make it look like robbery – or leave a cuff-link behind, to throw the police off the scent. It was over – and you couldn't bear it. So you dropped her, and left her. Now you've got her money, and you're running off to America. It might have all worked out, too - had Mr Sam not let his imagination run wild.'

He sat down heavily. For his part, Sam was subdued: it was probably the longest speech he'd ever heard Bradby make. He took a breath, and spoke up.

'It's not just my father who's suspicious, Florrie. He says I'm too trusting, but he can be wrong sometimes. Though when all's said and done, I never thought you could do what you...'

He broke off, for there was nothing more to be said. In silence he too sat down, to await the police.

They were the saddest minutes he had ever known.

TWENTY

Following the arrest of Florence Bates, some days passed in which The Great Albertini company took time to revise their plans. Briefly, they had found themselves in the limelight – not merely on account of Albert's fame, but for the fact that his son had been instrumental in solving the murder of Nancy Poole by her friend Miss Bates, the famous male impersonator. Mr Sam Vasey, the newspapers reported with glee, had faced down the knife-wielding harridan at her rooms in Lambeth, assisted by his employee, former soldier Mr Bradby Durrell. Only through courage and quick thinking had the two men managed to disarm the frenzied woman, before allowing the police to detain her. Now awaiting trial in Brixton Prison, Bates was refusing to speak; however, given the evidence which had been painstakingly amassed by Scotland Yard, the verdict seemed a foregone conclusion...

'*How are the mighty fallen.*'

Albert sat sober-faced in the drawing-room at Highgate, holding up the page that bore the headline. The piece, in a showbusiness newspaper, was regretful in tone, lamenting that someone as popular as Florrie Bates should have turned out to be a murderess. Two of the other men in the room – Sam and Bradby – remained silent; the third - Sergeant Drewe of the Metropolitan Police – gave a sigh. It was late Wednesday morning, and he had called in to express his thanks for Sam's help in solving what had been his most trying case.

'The woman will hang,' he said, looking round. 'I see no other outcome.'

Albert, who had been stunned by events since the previous Saturday, merely grunted; he was not in a forgiving mood. But Sam met the sergeant's gaze.

'It must be a relief to you,' he said. 'And now that the Okhrana men are taken…'

Drewe eyed him. 'Well - no such men exist, Mr Vasey. You'll recall the Russian Embassy denied knowing them? It seems they're quite unconcerned if the fellows are treated like any English criminals would be, and dealt with accordingly. They'll soon be forgotten. Miss Bates's execution will put everything else in the shade.'

Albert let out a breath. 'So, at long last this dreadful business is over. I may as well tell you, sergeant, that it's taken years off me.'

'And yet, he's eager to get back to work,' Sam said, with a wry look. 'Booking have started coming in again…'

'Of course they have,' Albert broke in. 'Why shouldn't they?'

The other men exchanged looks, but refrained from comment. And soon afterwards Drewe rose to take his leave, whereupon a half-smile appeared.

'I forgot to mention it: Inspector Maskell's up for promotion. The Commissioner has commended him personally, for letting Londoners sleep easy in their beds again.'

With that, he became business-like and made his farewells. Sam saw him to the door. As they shook hands, the sergeant gave him a warm look.

'If I thought you'd ever entertain the notion of joining us at the Yard,' he said, 'I'd recommend you without hesitation - but I know you won't. And I suspect that, despite your trials and tribulations managing your father, you rather enjoy it.'

'When all goes well, I do,' Sam admitted. 'But there are times…' he gave a shrug.

'Well, I'll let you get back to business,' Drewe said. 'I'm sure things will go well for you now…' he checked himself. 'I meant to say, I intend to bring my wife to one of The Great Albertini's shows soon. Any particular one you'd recommend?'

'Why – The Tivoli, of course,' Sam replied. 'Where else?'

With a wry smile, the sergeant put on his hat and went out.

Sam returned to the drawing-room to find Bradby and Albert on their feet, seemingly in some disagreement. As he entered, his father swung round to face him.

'He thinks I should do the mind-reading act again,' he said in exasperation. 'But how on earth is that possible without a Mirabel to memorise the signals? I've insisted we revive the vanishing bird-cage trick. Will you tell him, please?'

'I'm not going to tell him anything,' Sam answered. 'I have an appointment this afternoon. Or had you forgotten?'

'Ah… yes.' Albert frowned. 'Well, we'll leave it for tomorrow. In the meantime, I'll try and work a few things out.'

'A good idea, father,' Sam said. 'Now, can we have luncheon? I believe Alice has made dumplings.'

***

Shortly after two o'clock, he arrived at Waterloo Station and sought out the platform for trains to Southampton. The station was as busy and as noisy as always, porters wheeling laden trollies about amid the throng of passengers. Finally, having made his way towards the steaming, hissing locomotive, he saw a small crowd gathered beside the open door of a first-class carriage. Pushing his way through, he found the centre of attention: a familiar figure, brightly dressed and smiling. Miss Mattie Burns, The Triple-Jointed Terpsichorean Termagant and human cannonball, was bidding friends and loyal fans farewell. Beside her stood another figure, tall and elegant, if far more soberly dressed. As Sam drew near, they both saw him.

'Sammy!' Mattie spread her arms. As he tipped his hat, she drew close and embraced him. Standing back, she gestured about cheerfully.

'Quite a send-off, eh? I'm so touched, I could weep!'

'It's well-deserved,' Sam said with a smile. People swayed about them, chattering, but Louise Sidorov stood with eyes lowered. Close by was a pile of cases and boxes, and a porter had arrived to take them aboard. Before Sam could say more, Mattie seized his arm.

'I read the papers,' she murmured, forcing him to bend close. 'I'm mighty glad it's over at last - even though I can hardly believe it. You did well, Sammy… you're a trouper.'

Embarrassed, Sam looked away – whereupon with a sigh, Mattie let go of him. 'I'd better let you have a moment with Louise,' she said. 'Pass my respects to Albert – I guess you and he have a lot of work to do, eh?'

And with that she put a finger to her lips, pressed it to his mouth and turned away to say her last good-byes. As the little group closed about her, Sam stepped aside to greet Louise.

'I am so glad you came,' she said quickly. 'I would have been sad not to see you again – but from what I have heard, it may be that we can meet in America. Is it true? Is your father going to tour there?'

For a moment, Sam hesitated; nobody, apart from Conrad de Brun, yet knew of the decision Albert had taken the evening before. He was about to speak – but seeing his expression, the woman took a breath.

'So… it is not true.' For a second her face fell, though she mastered herself quickly.

'Sadly not…we won't be leaving these shores just now,' Sam told her. 'My father is eager to rebuild - I might say, to repair his reputation here. It matters more to him than going to America, no matter how lucrative it may be.' He managed a smile. 'He's a Londoner through and through… as are we both, in fact.'

'Yes, I understand.' She made an effort to smile in return. Their eyes met… he might have spoken, but knew it was of no use.

'I cannot say that I will return to London,' Louise said at last. 'Which is a pity… but just now, I am content. Mattie is my friend for life… I cannot thank her enough. And I could say the same to you, Monsieur Vasey - *mon cher*. But then, I think you understand too.'

With that she put out a gloved hand, and Sam took it. He held it for a moment, while somewhere a whistle blew, and the farewell party stepped back from the carriage.

He released her and watched as she climbed aboard, following Mattie. People waved and called out, handkerchiefs fluttered, and a guard came up to slam the door. With a great hiss of steam and a clank of wheels, the locomotive began to ease forward, puffing clouds of grey smoke.

Sam did not wait with the others to see it leave the station. Instead, he turned away and walked back to the concourse, finally making his way outside into autumn sunshine. Quickening his pace, he moved through the afternoon crowds, seeking a cab to take him back to Highgate, and to the work that awaited him

He had a show to organise, and The Great Albertini was not known for his patience.

Printed in Great Britain
by Amazon

76185661R00128